The Muse
A Short Story

and

The Federal Reserve
Audit, Amend, or Abolish

Tighe Taylor, JD

Copyright © 2025 Tighe Taylor

All rights reserved. No part of this book may be reproduced or transmitted in any form or by any means, electronic or mechanical, including photocopying, recording or by any information storage and retrieval system without permission in writing from the publisher.

Black Cat Publishing – Sherman Oaks, CA
Paperback ISBN: 979-8-218-68991-9
eBook ISBN: 979-8-3493-5294-2
Library of Congress Control Number: 2025910280
The Muse (A Short Story) and The Federal Reserve (Audit, Amend, or Abolish)
Author: Tighe Taylor
Digital distribution | 2025
Paperback | 2025

This is a work of fiction. The characters, names, incidents, places, and dialogue are products of the author's imagination, and are not to be construed as real.

Published in the United States by New Book Authors Publishing

Previous Books by Tighe Taylor

The Tragic Death of Marina Habe
The Kidnapping of Tammy Fitzgerald, Second Edition
The Kidnapping of Taylor Shaw
The Kidnaping of Isabel Miller
The Kidnapping of Crystal Covington
The Constitutional Convention
(and other stories)

Dedicated to

Yuki Terayama,

For her patient listening.

Table of Contents

The Federal Reserve – Audit, Amend, or Abolish 1
The Muse – A Short Story 93
About the Author 154

The Federal Reserve
Audit, Amend, or Abolish

Table of Contents

Preface xi

Chapter 1 – The National Debt 1

Chapter 2 – History of Banking 19

Chapter 3 – The Federal Reserve 35

Preface

We offer a look into the origins, workings, and future of the Federal Reserve system so that we may evaluate the benefits of the system with a view towards keeping or abandoning it. We examine its pitfalls and historical objections.

We provide background with chapters on the national debt and the history of banking in the United States in an effort to better understand the subject.

In Chapter 1, we start with the national debt. We introduce the concepts of printing money, gold-backed money, fiat money, and the Federal Reserve's ability to create money out of thin air. We discuss the Constitutional aspect of assigning value to money.

We show the various programs that the federal government is required to conduct, such as defense spending, Social Security, Medicare, and government pensions, noting that these programs are required to be carried out even if the money for them is not immediately available.

In a year during which the government conducts its programs but lacks the revenue to pay for them, it is said to be running a **deficit**. When all of the deficits are added together, they total the **national debt.**

We discuss public vs. intragovernmental debt, both of which are considered part of the national debt, even though intragovernmental debt is only a debt owed by one part of the government to another.

We show who owns the national debt and discuss the relationship between the Gross Domestic Product and the national debt.

When the government borrows money, **both the principal and the interest become part of the national debt. 37 to 40 percent of the income tax collected goes to paying the interest alone.**

We show what percentage of the government's revenue is paid by whom. Taxpayers pay nearly half while corporations pay only 11 percent.

We discuss debt ceiling and the methods used to postpone its operation.

In Chapter 2, we discuss the history of banking in the United States. We present a table showing the six primary banking institutions which existed between 1782 and 1913, including the last, the Federal Reserve.

We discuss the First and Second Banks of the United States. Though they were both quite large and as such did have an effect on the banking system, their operation was more similar to a commercial bank than a central bank, as they did not make monetary policy. The First Bank was allowed to expire in 1811. In 1832, President Andrew Jackson vetoed the bill to recharter the bank, and its charter expires in 1836.

In the 1860s, banking was controlled by the National Banking Act. It provided for a fairly stable currency, the National Bank Note, which was backed by U.S. Treasury securities. Its backing contributed to the National Bank Note being considered inelastic, as it was unable to expand or contract with the needs of business.

Under the Act, branch banking was not favored. As a result, reserves were scattered around the country in one-unit banks, making access to reserves more difficult.

Further, when access to reserves became necessary, because the currency was inelastic, the banks had to either sell stock or decline to make loans.

Between 1863 and 1913, there were several banking panics, including the Panic of 1907. Depositors, fearing that their bank would not have sufficient cash to repay their deposits, made mass withdrawals or runs on the bank leading to bank failures.

Senator Nelson Aldrich visited Europe and studied their banking practices. He was persuaded to consider a central bank for the United States. He led a group to Jekyll Island, an island off the coast of Georgia, to discuss a central banking system. The result of this meeting was the Aldrich Plan. In 1912, Woodrow Wilson was elected President. Though he opposed the Aldrich plan, he did feel that banking reform was needed.

The Aldrich Plan was not adopted. However, the plan favored by President Wilson, the Federal Reserve system, was. The Aldrich Plan gave power over banking to the bankers. The Federal Reserve system, at the insistence of President Wilson, gave power over banking to a government Board, the Federal Reserve Board. It was passed in 1913.

Chapter 3 goes on to explain the operation of the Federal Reserve.

In its Preamble, the Federal Reserve Act outlines its primary goals which were to establish Federal Reserve Banks, to provide an elastic currency, and to allow the rediscounting of commercial paper for bank loans.

Because of an aversion to a single central bank, initially the Federal Reserve Act divided the country into 12 districts with a central bank, known as a Reserve Bank, in each district. All of the national banks and as many of the State banks as wished could join the Fed as a member bank, provided that they purchased stock and provided reserves.

Member banks could borrow from one another at the fed funds rate. If a bank cannot borrow from another bank due to credit problems, it could borrow from the Reserve Bank at the Discount Rate at the Discount Window, making the Fed the Lender of Last Resort. At the Discount Window, banks could pledge discounted commercial paper as collateral.

The Act also provided for an elastic currency, the Federal Reserve Note, which could expand or contract with the needs of business. The Fed could only issue 2 ½ times the amount of gold that it held, which lessened inflation.

It might be interesting to note that because of all of the

banking panics, the original purpose of the Federal Reserve was to provide banks with emergency cash to pay their depositors. From this humble beginning, the Fed would go on to manage the economy for an entire country.

After World War I, the Fed began buying and selling securities. It found, some say by accident, that by so doing, it would affect the general economy. When buying and selling securities, the Fed was acting under its authority to conduct Open Market Operations within Section 14 of the Act.

The Fed's initial monetary tools included setting the Discount Rate and changing bank reserves. By the 1920s, its primary tool became Open Market Operations. We should keep in mind that the Discount Window is still used today and was used for the 2008 financial crisis and the COVID-19 pandemic.

With Open Market Operations, the Fed would buy securities from the bank with money printed out of thin air. Rather than giving the money to the bank, it would add to the bank's reserves. This would increase reserves, produce more money to lend, lower interest rates, and increase the money supply, all of which would stimulate the economy.

When the Fed sold securities, it would take money from the bank's reserves. This would leave less money in the bank's reserves, which would raise interest rates, and cool the economy.

From the 1920s until 1970, the Fed used Open Market Operations to manage the economy.

In 1970, the Fed changed and began to manage the economy with the fed funds rate.

From 1979 until 1982, the new Board Chairman, Paul Volcker, attempted to manage the economy with the money supply.

When that failed, in 1982, the Fed returned to using the fed funds rate, which it still uses.

When using the fed funds rate, the Fed sets a target range for the rate and steers the rate to the target range.

The Fed did not, and does not now, actually set the fed funds rate, only a target range for that rate.

From 1970 until 2008 (except for 1979 to 1982), the Fed used Open Market Operations to steer the fed funds rate to its target.

In 2008, with the 2008 financial crisis, the Fed reduced the fed funds rate to near zero. The Fed was forced to use Quantitative Easing. It made large-scale purchases of long-term securities, mortgaged backed securities, and assets, placing the purchase price into bank reserves. This gave the bank ample rather than limited reserves.

Because of this, Congress allowed the Fed to pay interest on reserve balances (IORB). Thereafter, interest on reserve balances, an administered rate, was used to steer the fed funds rate to its target.

In short, to steer the fed funds rate to its target, before 2008, the Fed used Open Market Operations, and from 2008 until present, it uses interest on reserve balances.

Presently, the Federal Open Market Committee (FOMC) meets eight times a year and, based on its financial data, decides whether the economy requires stimulation or cooling.

If it requires stimulation, it will set a new target range for the fed funds rate below the existing rate to reduce interest rates. If the economy requires cooling, it will set a new target range above the existing rate to raise interest rates.

The Chairman of the Federal Reserve Board will announce the new fed funds rate.

If the economy needed stimulation, the Fed Chairman will announce that the new fed funds rate will be lower than the existing rate. If the economy needed cooling, the Fed Chairman will announce that the new fed funds rate will be higher than the existing rate.

The change is typically announced in terms of basis points with the new rate being either 25 or 50 basis points below or above the existing rate. 25 basis points is one-quarter of one percent. 50 basis points is one-half of one percent.

Commencing before the enactment of Federal Reserve system and continuing until today, many in and out of government have criticized the Federal Reserve as having too much power over the nation's economy. Much of this criticism has been centered around two things: (1) the Fed's ability to create new money and give it to the banks of its choosing, and (2) the fact that to fight off recession, the Fed has only inflated the currency and increased the money supply with its attendant devaluation of the dollar.

Chapter 3 sets forth many of the arguments for and against the Federal Reserve and some of the ways that the system may be audited, amended, or abolished.

Chapter 1
The National Debt

"We don't have a trillion-dollar debt because we haven't taxed enough; we have a trillion-dollar debt because we spend too much."

Ronald Reagan,
40th President of the United States

Introduction

Economics in the United States is relatively complicated. This is due in part to the fact that the principles are complex. However, it is also partly due to the fact that the people advancing the principles are not as forthcoming as they might be about its actual operation.

The national debt and the Federal Reserve are separate items; however, there are some areas of overlap which are seldom reported.

As we all know, the United States is in serious debt, approximately 38 trillion dollars at the time of this writing. As we will see as we progress, the Federal Reserve has the power to create money out of thin air and has done so several times over the years.

This brings us to our first question: If we are able to create so much money, why not print enough money to get out of debt?

The answer: The national debt and the federal reserve do not work together in this way.

When the government, the primary creator of debt, creates

debt, it needs to borrow money to repay it, including interest. This means that when the government borrows, it has to repay both the principal and interest. As a result, both the principal and interest are added to our national debt. The result becomes even more onerous when we consider that presently that the interest payment alone on the national debt consumes 37 to 40 percent of the income tax collected.

Before proceeding further, allow us to define three concepts which should help our understanding; they are "printing" money, "backed" currency, "Open Market Operations."

Printing Money – Economic writers, in a bout of silliness, will often maintain that the Federal Reserve does not print money. They say that printing money is done by the U.S. Treasury. Yes, this is true. But they are referring to the physical act of making currency. The physical act of "printing" money on a printing press is done by Treasury. However, the act of "creating" money where there was none before is done by the Federal Reserve; this is the money creation of which we will be speaking.

To avoid any misunderstandings, when discussing the Federal Reserve, we will use the term "printing" money to include "creating" money by the Federal Reserve. To print money out of thin air, the Federal Reserve needs legal authorization which it obtains from Section 14 of the Federal Reserve Act.

> "... we have delivered to a secretive body the privilege of creating money out of thin air; if you or I, did it, we'd be called counterfeiters, so why have we legalized counterfeiting? But the economic reasons are overwhelming: the Federal Reserve is the creature that destroys value.
>
> Ron Paul,
> **Member, United States House of Representatives**

Backed Currency – For years, currency in the United States was "backed," that is, the paper currency was backed by an asset such as gold, silver, or Treasury securities.

In this way, only as much paper currency for which there was backing could be issued. Obviously, if only backed paper currency could be issued, there would be less currency in circulation and, therefore, less inflation.

When the Federal Reserve Act was passed, it included a currency known as a Federal Reserve Note. Initially, the volume of Federal Reserve Notes which could be made available was limited to 2 1/2 times the amount of the gold held by the Fed. This was designed to combat inflation. In June 1945, the volume of notes available was increased to 4 times the amount of gold held by the Fed.

In 1971, we went off of the gold standard during the Nixon Administration. As a result, today's currency is not backed by metals or securities. It is only backed by the full faith and credit of the United States.

Currency issued with no backing is known as "fiat" money. As should appear fairly obvious, fiat money is subject to serious inflation as it has no backing requirement to lessen the amount of currency which may be placed into circulation at any given time. Fiat currency has precipitated the downfall of several civilizations.

In the past, fiat money was used during emergencies, such as the Civil War. During the Civil War a species of fiat money known as "greenbacks" was used.

Currency backing in the United States appears as follows:
1792 to 1862 – Bimetal backing, both gold and silver.
1863 to 1879 – With the Civil War, "greenbacks" with no backing.
1879 to 1933 – Full Gold Standard.
1934 to 1971 – Partial Gold Standard; and
1971 to present – Fiat money when President Nixon took us off of the Gold Standard.

Open Market Operations - In the late 19th and early 20th Centuries, banks in the United States experienced considerable turmoil. Depositors, fearing for the safety of their funds, would withdraw their money rather than lose it. This led to "runs" on the banks and bank failures.

In 1913, Congress, with the encouragement of then President Woodrow Wilson, passed the Federal Reserve Act to help stabilize banking. The Act created 12 Federal Reserve districts, each with its own Federal Reserve Bank. Existing national banks were required to join the Fed, and State banks could elect to join by paying the appropriate fees. The banks which joined were known as member banks.

The Federal Reserve Act provided a reserve banking system. Member banks were required to hold a certain amount in reserve in Federal Reserve Notes in their vaults or at the local Reserve Bank. A member bank could borrow from another member bank at the fed funds rate.

If a bank was unable to borrow from another bank due to poor credit, it could borrow from the Fed at its Discount Window at the slightly higher Discount Rate, a rate set by the Fed. This made the Fed the Lender of Last Resort.

The Fed remained a lender for its first five years of operation, from 1913 until after the conclusion of World War I. To support the War and its aftermath, the Fed began buying and selling securities. When it did so, it was found, some say by accident, that the general economy was affected.

The Federal Reserve Act specifically provided for the Fed to act as a lender. It did not, however, provide for the Fed to act as the maker of monetary policy or to become the pursuer of a dual mandate of price stability and full employment.

After World War I, the Fed began to emphasize its activities as a maker of monetary policy rather than as a lender.

In the 1920s, the Fed began to adjust its Discount Rate. Initially, the Fed used interest earned from lending to member banks at the Discount Rate as a primary source of income to cover its operating expenses as there was no robust market for government securities to conduct Open Market Operations. The Fed's primary tool for providing liquidity was the Discount Window where member banks pledged commercial or agricultural loans to obtain cash paying the Discount Rate. However, as things progressed, the Fed began using Open Market Operations.

With Open Market Operations, the Fed creates money out of thin air and purchases securities. When it does so, it does not give the cash to the bank but, instead, credits the bank's reserve account.

Throughout the 1920's, the Great Depression, and World War II, fed funds trading remained fairly thin, and the fed funds rate remained well below the discount rate.

To manage the economy, the Fed used Open Market Operations.

For example, in 1924 and 1927, the Fed purchased securities when the economy went into recession, which moved the economy out of recession.

In 1928, the Fed sold securities to tighten the economy to discourage stock market speculation. It has been contended that this moved the economy from recession to depression, the Great Depression.

After World War II, as trading volume increased, the fed funds rate began to become more visible. By the 1960s, the Fed was actively monitoring the fed funds rate to gauge money market conditions.

By 1970, the Federal Open Market Committee began using the fed funds rate to manage the economy. It began setting a target range for the fed funds rate.

In the 1970s, the Fed, while using the fed funds rate to manage the economy, used Open Market Operations to steer the fed funds rate to its target, and began pursuing its dual mandate of low unemployment and stable prices.

After the 2008 financial crisis. While still using the fed funds rate to manage the economy, the Fed changed its method of steering the fed funds rate to its target.

After the 2008 financial crisis, the Fed reduced the fed funds rate to near zero. As a result, it could no longer adjust the fed funds rate to stimulate the economy.

With this being the case, the Fed was forced to resort to Quantitative Easing.

With Quantitative Easing, the Fed, with money created out of thin air, purchased long-term securities (as opposed to short term), mortgage-backed securities, and other assets, and credited the money to the banks' reserves.

This greatly increased the quantity of reserves in the banking system. This created a situation where reserves became ample. Thereafter, Congress allowed interest to be paid on reserve balances.

Rather than adjusting the fed funds rate by the Open Market Operations of buying and selling securities, the Fed began to adjust the interest rate based on the interest rate on reserve balances. As an administered rate, the Fed could adjust the interest on reserve balances and use it to ensure that the fed funds rate stayed within its target.

In summary, from 1913 to 1918, the Fed acted primarily as a lender. By the 1920s, the Fed engaged in monetary policy firstly with Open Market Operations and then in 1970 with changes to the fed funds rate. The fed funds rate was steered from 1970 to 2008 by Open Market Operations and from 2008 to present by the interest rate set on reserve balances.

It might be interesting to note that though being Lender of Last Resort was one of the original duties delegated to the Fed because a purpose of the Federal Reserve Act was to supply money to banks to curtail bank panics, as time progressed, the lender feature was not used extensively until the 2008 financial crisis and the COVID-19 pandemic, where its use was, in effect, resurrected, as we will see.

Constitutional Authority

The Appropriations Clause, Article I, Section 9 of the United States Constitution, creates a legislative duty under which Congress controls federal spending. Congress is anointed with the "power of the purse."

The Appropriations Clause enjoins the President from spending funds unless those funds are appropriated by Congress. If Congress could not limit the President from spending, the constitutional grant to Congress to raise taxes or borrow money would be meaningless as the President could compel taxing and borrowing merely by his own spending.

Of course, there are emergencies during which the President might spend even when constitutionally prohibited, particularly to provide for the national security. Further, it would seem as if Congress would be obligated to provide funds for the President to carry out his constitutional duties set forth in Article II.

With the Appropriations Clause, an appropriation would specify the amount of money which may be spent together with the powers, activities, and purposes (the "object) for which the money might be used.

Congress has often authorized agencies to obligate federal funds to federal agencies which have not yet been appropriated; this does not violate the Appropriations Clause.

Other statutes authorize Congress to engage in "backdoor" spending such as where Congress authorizes federal agencies to engage in spending. This would include interest payments on the national debt.

Statutory entitlement programs such as Social Security and unemployment benefits are generally funded by permanent appropriations contained within the statute creating the program itself.

The Federal Reserve has been given permanent, plenary authority to set its own budget, without Congressional oversight, to allow it to maintain political independence.

Programs that the Government Runs

The Preamble to the United States Constitution states that the purpose of the federal government is "... to establish Justice, insure [sic] domestic Tranquility, provide for the common defense, promote the general Welfare, and secure the Blessings of Liberty to ourselves and our Posterity." To accomplish these purposes, uninterrupted funding of certain programs and services is necessary.

The following are some of the important programs and services which the government is charged with providing:
1. Income Security – This would include programs such as unemployment compensation, federal employee retirement and disability benefits, nutritional support, etc.
2. Social Security – Retirement and disability insurance.
3. Health – Programs related to health care services other than Medicare.
4. National Defense – Military activities.
5. Medicare – Medical programs for seniors over 65 and younger qualifying individuals with certain disabilities.

As it is necessary for the government to keep these programs running on an uninterrupted basis, it will be required to do so even when it does not have sufficient funds on hand. In other words, to keep these programs running, the government will spend more than it takes in.

If in a particular year the government spends more than it takes in, it is said to be running a deficit. All of the deficits added together constitute the national debt.

Public vs. Intragovernmental Debt (Gross Debt vs Net Debt)

The term "net" or "public" debt is what the government owes the public, including the Federal Reserve, foreign countries, and individual investors. A chart is included below.

The term "intragovernmental debt" refers to what one part of the government owes to another part of the government. This includes money held in government trusts such as Social Security and government retirement accounts. Intragovernmental debt has no economic significance.

The term "gross debt" refers to the public debt plus the intragovernmental debt.

The term "national debt," rather than referring only to the net or public debt, refers to the gross debt. As a result, the term national debt includes intragovernmental debt.

Of the national debt, 79 percent is public debt while 21 percent is intragovernmental debt.

When we hear that the national debt is 38 trillion dollars, the figure unknowingly sets forth the gross debt which includes the public debt plus the intragovernmental debt. It includes, at least partly, a debt with no economic significance, the intragovernmental debt.

An example of why the gross debt figure is misleading may be seen with Social Security. Let us assume that in a given year Social Security runs at a surplus. Social Security sends the surplus to Treasury. In return, Treasury sends securities to Social Security. The securities that Social Security receives are exactly offset by new intragovernmental debt incurred by Treasury. It is a debt which is not actually a debt but only money owed by one branch of the government to another.

When the "debt ceiling" is reached, the debt limit is determined by the gross debt which includes both the public debt and the intragovernmental debt. Intragovernmental debt should not be included in determining the debt limit; however, it is.

Most economists feel that the public debt is more meaningful as it reflects the amount that the Treasury has borrowed from outsiders including the Federal Reserve, individual investors, mutual funds, and foreign countries such as Japan, China, and the UK.

The debt owed to the Federal Reserve is considered public and not intragovernmental because the Federal Reserve is, at least in theory, separate from the government.

The Federal Reserve buys and sells Treasury securities as a means of executing monetary policy. Due to the COVID-19 pandemic, its purchases became extensive causing the Federal Reserve to own over 34 percent of the public debt. The Fed's holding is not an intragovernmental debt as the Federal Reserve is technically independent of the government.

The following shows who owns the net debt and in what percentages:

Federal Reserve	34.85 percent
Foreign countries	23.35 percent
Other investors	16.28 percent
Mutual funds	10.76 percent
State and local governments	4.94 percent
Depository	4.86 percent
Private pensions	1.80 percent
Insurance Companies	1.40 percent
State and local government pensions	1.24 percent
U.S. savings bonds	.51 percent

National Debt to Gross Domestic Product Ratio

To understand the national debt, it may be interesting to compare the national debt to the gross domestic product. The gross domestic product reflects the government's ability to pay down the national debt. This ratio is achieved by dividing the national debt by the gross domestic product. If the debt to GDP ratio is above 77 percent, investors should start to worry about whether the country will be able to pay the national debt. The United States began incurring debt even before it became a nation as it needed to borrow money from France and the Netherlands to win its independence from Great Britain. The Continental Congress, the governing body before Congress, did not have the power to tax. As a result, the national debt continued to grow.

According to Alexander Hamilton, the first Secretary of the Treasury, by 1790, the national debt was $75,000,000. At that time, the debt to GDP ratio was 30 percent. The growing economy helped to decrease the debt to GDP ratio to below 10 percent, until the War of 1812.

With the War of 1812, the country had to go deeply into debt to fight the British again. (As we will see, wars are the most significant contributors to the national debt and have fueled the interest payments enjoyed by the banks for decades.)

By the time that Andrew Jackson took office in 1828, the national debt was $58,000,000. By selling off federally owned land in the west, Jackson paid off all of the national debt by 1835. Unfortunately, within a year, an economic recession led the government to start borrowing; the government would never be debt free again. Due to the Civil War, by 1866, the national debt increased to $2.76 billion. Economic growth in the late 1800s, coupled with inflation, decreased the debt to GDP ratio. However, after World War I, the debt to GDP ratio hit 33 percent with a national debt of $25 billion.

World War I saw a major shift in the control of the national debt when Congress agreed to give the Treasury Department more flexibility, allowing it to raise money through the sale of securities. Though Congress lost the right to approve or disapprove of each individual sale, it did retain the right to set an overall limit on borrowing known as the debt ceiling.

Congress has since raised or lowered the debt ceiling, the maximum amount of outstanding debt that the federal government can legally incur, numerous times. The national debt grew dramatically as the economy went into recession and the size, scope, and role of the federal government expanded during the Great Depression and the New Deal in the 1930s.

When World War II came, the debt to GDP ratio rose above 77 percent for the first time in the nation's history, reaching 113 percent (an all-time record) by the end of the war. After World War II, the booming post war economy saw a rapid rise in the GDP. By 1974, the debt to GDP ratio went as low as 24 percent.

Due to recession and rising interest rates, significant permanent tax cuts during Ronald Reagan's first term, and increased spending on both defense and social programs caused the debt to GDP ratio to increase to nearly 50 percent by the early 1990s.

Economic growth in the late 1990s combined with tax increases under both Presidents George H.W. Bush and Bill Clinton helped to reduce the national debt. By 2001, the debt to GDP ratio was reduced to 33 percent.

Unfortunately, increased military spending after the terrorist attack of 9/11, the tax cuts under George W. Bush, and the arrival of the Great Recession caused the GDP to fall rapidly. These factors led business activities and tax revenues to shrink. Even with the nation's economic recovery and the end of the war in Iraq and the draw-down of the war in Afghanistan, the U.S. debt to GDP ratio remained above 100 since 2013. During 2017, the total national debt passed $20 trillion for the first time in the nation's history, with debt levels continuing to rise.

In early 2018, an analysis by the nonpartisan Committee for a Responsible Federal Budget concluded that the tax and spend legislation passed by Congress under President Trump was on track to push the country's debt to GDP ratio to heights not seen since the end of World War II. The report stated that if the tax cuts and spending remained permanent, the national debt could pass $33 trillion or 113 percent of GDP. It did so by 2024.

The COVID-19 pandemic has impacted national debts around the world. Additional economic stimulus packages could push the national debt even higher.

We have learned that wars and social spending programs contribute greatly to the national debt. **When a country is over 38 trillion dollars in debt, to discharge its constitutional duties to provide a defense and maintain the general welfare, it will have no alternative but to borrow.**

Wars are the greatest panacea for bankers since the advent of the teller window. As a government does not have sufficient resources on hand to undertake a war, it must borrow. And when it borrows, it has to repay both the principal and interest. Generally, interest payments on the national debt consume 37 to 40 percent of all personal income tax collected. Elon Musk has been quoted as saying that he is glad that the income tax that he is now paying "goes directly to important things like interest on past government incompetence."

Federal Government Revenue

In fiscal 2024, the federal government collected revenue from four primary sources:

1. Personal income tax: 49 percent ($2.4 trillion)
2. Payroll tax (Social Security, Medicare): 35 percent ($1.7 trillion)
3. Corporate income tax: 11 percent ($530 billion)
4. Customs, duties (tariffs), estate, and excise taxes: 5 percent (253 billion)

When we consider the above, it becomes clear that people are expected to shoulder nearly half of the tax burden.

The numbers look like this:
1. The top 1 percent of people pay 45 percent of the income tax collected.

2. The top 10 percent of people pay 76 percent of the income tax collected.
3. The top 50 percent of people pay 97 percent of the income tax collected.
4. The bottom 50 percent of people pay 3 percent of the income tax collected.
5. The top 20 percent of people pay more of the income tax collected than the rest of the taxpayers combined.

In short, when the government lacks the revenue to fund an essential program, it runs the program anyway, incurring a deficit which becomes part of the national debt. From the table above, we see that the largest payors of the national debt are taxpayers. Therefore, programs are essentially paid for by the taxpayers.

At our founding, under Alexander Hamilton's plan, duties and tariffs were supposed to pay for the bulk of the cost of running the government. There was no mention of an income tax in the original Constitution. The income tax was not added until the Constitution was amended in 1913 with the 16th Amendment. Coincidentally, this was the same year that the Federal Reserve Act passed. Whereas the initial plan was for tariffs and duties to pay for the operation of the government, presently, tariffs and duties account for less than 2 percent of revenue.

The Debt Ceiling

Congress has authorized trillions of dollars in spending over the last decade causing the national debt to nearly triple since 2009. In 1917, Congress created the debt ceiling. The debt ceiling sets the maximum amount of federal debt that the government may incur. When the debt ceiling has been reached, the government will have to shut down, pass a new full year budget, or pass a continuing resolution to raise or suspend the debt ceiling.

A new full year budget requires a vote of both the House of Representatives and the Senate. This vote would require a majority vote in the House and now, under the Filibuster Rule, a super-majority vote of 60 in the Senate. In 1974, Congress enacted the Congressional Budget Act of 1974. This Act provides for reconciliation which allows expedited treatment for certain tax, spending, and debt limit legislation. More importantly, a reconciliation bill is not subject to the Filibuster Rule. For a reconciliation bill to pass, a majority vote would be required in the House, but only a simple majority of 51 votes would be required in the Senate, rather than the super-majority of 60.

Since 1960, Congress has increased the debt ceiling 78 times. 49 increases have been implemented under Republican Presidents, and 29 have been implemented under Democrat Presidents. Because raising the debt ceiling is required for the government to continue to pay its bills, for much of the past century, raising the debt ceiling has been a routine procedure. The Treasury Department reached the debt ceiling of $31.4 trillion in January 2023. After months of debate, Congress voted to suspend the debt ceiling until January 2025. In January 2025, the debt limit was reinstated at $36.1 trillion, the amount of the outstanding debt at that time. In 2025, Congress was unable to pass a full fiscal year budget. Fortunately, to keep the government open, in March 2025, both houses of Congress passed a continuing resolution averting a government shutdown through the end of fiscal 2025, which was September 30, 2025.

The National Debt and the Federal Reserve

For several years, the national debt has been larger than the Country's gross domestic product. The debt to GDP ratio puts debt into relative terms by comparing debt to the nation's ability to repay that debt, which is the gross domestic product.

The debt as a share of GDP has gone through three main growth phases in recent decades. The government ran large budget deficits during the Reagan-Bush years of the 1980s. The 2008 financial crisis and the COVID-19 pandemic caused the debt to spike to an all-time high of 134 percent of GDP. The ratio has come down, but it remains well above pre-pandemic levels.

Before the COVID-19 pandemic, the largest percentage of the national debt belonged to intragovernmental holdings such as Social Security, Medicare, and retirement accounts.

Servicing the national debt and the interest on the national debt is one of the government's largest expenses. Net interest payments on the debt are estimated to be a total of $395 billion or 6.8 percent of all federal outlays and is significantly more than it will spend on veterans' benefits, education, disaster relief, agriculture, science and space programs, foreign aid, and environmental protection.

Today, the Federal Reserve is the largest holder of U.S. debt. While throughout its history, the Fed regularly bought and sold Treasuries to execute monetary policy, the 2008 Financial Crisis and the COVID-19 pandemic required additional buying.

By March 2020, the Fed held 20 percent of the national debt whereas 10 years earlier, its share of the debt was under 11 percent. **Looking at our table, we see that presently the Federal Reserve owns approximately 35 percent of the national debt. The Federal Reserve has always taken the position that it is not funded by the taxpayers (the payors of the national debt) but is funded by the interest it earns on the securities that it holds. The Fed creates money out of thin air** which it uses to purchase securities.

When the Fed purchases securities, the money realized is not paid in cash but is injected into the banking system by crediting bank reserves; this also increases the money supply.

The Fed maintains that it buys and sells government securities only to influence interest rates and the money supply and that these transactions are merely its method of conducting monetary policy. The position is that even though the Fed purchased securities and owns the largest percentage of the public national debt, it is not connected to that debt because it purchased the securities only as a method of conducting monetary policy and not a way to finance the deficit.

The Fed's purchase of securities is made independently of the government's borrowing decisions. The Fed's only mandate is to achieve maximum employment and stable prices.

It might be interesting to note that the portion of the national debt owned by the Fed is included in the public rather than the intragovernmental debt category. This is because the Federal Reserve is considered, technically, to not be part of the government but is independent of it. As a result, it is not the case of one branch of the government owing another, such as with Social Security. In short, the Federal Reserve buys securities only as a method of managing the economy.

Conclusion

We have seen that the government is responsible for the defense of the nation and providing for the general welfare of the country.

We have seen that there is public debt and intragovernmental debt. Public debt is debt owed to the public. Intragovernmental debt is debt owed by one branch of the government to another, such as Social Security.

We have seen that taxpayers pay nearly half of the national debt.

We have seen that when the government is in debt, to provide for today's taxpayers, it must borrow money. When this is done, it must add the principal and interest to the national debt. The interest added has become a significant part of the national debt.

We have seen that when the government borrows today to pay for programs for taxpayers, it must either increase taxes or push those taxes down the road to be paid by our children and grandchildren.

To this we say:

> **"Blessed are the young, for they shall inherit our nation's debts."**
>
> **Herbert Hoover,
> 31st President of the United States**

Chapter 2
History of Banking

"I believe that banking institutions are more dangerous to our liberties than standing armies."

Thomas Jefferson,
3rd President of the United States

U. S. Banking History

Beginning in 1782 and extending up to and including the passage of the Federal Reserve Act in 1913, there were six significant banking institutions in the United States. They were:

1. The Bank of North America (1782).
2. The First Bank of the United States (1791-1811).
3. The Second Bank of the United States (1816-1836).
4. Free Banking (1837-1862).
5. The National Banking Act (1863-1907); and
6. The Federal Reserve System (1913 to present).

Central banks existed in Europe prior to American Independence. Initially, however, they were not favored by most people in the United States. When evaluating American history, it is important to remember that there were vast differences among the various parts of this country. The north was primarily a commercial district while the south remained primarily agricultural. A central bank was considered to be of value to the north but not necessarily to the south. The two men who best epitomized these differences were Alexander Hamilton, the first Secretary of the Treasury under George Washington, and Thomas Jefferson, the first Secretary of State in the same Administration.

Mr. Hamilton saw the United States as a potential commercial center. He developed a plan to help the country grow financially. His plan included tariffs, excise taxes and duties, a national currency, and a national ban.

Mr. Jefferson, on the other hand, saw the United States as being based on agriculture, and viewed large cities as areas of corruption. He looked at industrial growth and the concentration of economic power in institutions such as banks as threats to liberty. To Jefferson, banks encouraged people to speculate rather than make money from honest labor.

Mr. Jefferson felt that banks chartered by the national government would operate branches in all of the States and would present unfair competition to State chartered banks that operated in one place, receiving fewer federal advantages.

Also, Mr. Jefferson did not think that the Constitution gave Congress the power to create a national bank. Tensions arose concerning the role of government in banking. Those who had capital wanted conservative monetary policies to safeguard it. Those who needed capital favored more liberal policies with easy access to credit, even at the risk of encouraging inflation.

Proponents and opponents of central banking have clung to their differences over many years with the northern part of the country favoring central banks as necessary to establishing a commercial base, and with the southern part of the country opposing central banks as an impingement on States' rights, as not absolutely necessary for agriculture, as running contrary to interest rates being set by the marketplace, and as generally being contrary to the American spirit of individual freedom.

Pre-Federal Reserve Banks

The Bank of North America 1782

In 1782, before the Constitution was ratified and based on a plan presented by Robert Morris and recommended by Alexander Hamilton, the Bank of North America was founded in Philadelphia. It was the country's first de facto central bank. The Pennsylvania government objected to its privileges and reincorporated it under State law, making it no longer a national bank.

The First Bank of the United States 1791-1811

Shortly after the Constitution was finalized, the new Congress asked Alexander Hamilton to devise an economic plan. He developed a plan wherein all of the duties collected from foreign governments would flow to the new central government and not to the States which levied them. All duties so collected were to be used by the new Congress to pay the debts owed by the federal and State governments and to the rich colonists who made contributions to the Revolutionary War. The money owed to the rich colonists was evidenced by something known as a "public security."

All debts were to be repaid at face value to preserve the credit of the new nation. (Some writers have argued that the Constitution itself was enacted so that the rich colonists would be repaid in full for their public securities rather have their public securities repaid at a discounted rate, a method which was favored by many.) In addition to collecting duties, Mr. Hamilton's plan included high protective tariffs, subsidies for local businesses, and a central bank.

In 1789, the Constitution was ratified, replacing the Articles of Confederation. Questions arose as to whether the Constitution allowed Congress to operate a national bank. Notwithstanding this, in 1791, during the first Washington Administration, Mr. Hamilton moved his economic plan, including the First Bank of the United States, through Congress by accepting a compromise with Southern lawmakers by which they would support his financial plan if he agreed to move the national capital from its temporary location in New York to a Southern location on the Potomac. The First Bank of the United States came into existence with the signature of George Washington.

The First Bank of the United States had a charter of 20 years, from 1791 until 1811.

It did not do well as it was partly owned by foreigners, and it was not solely responsible for the country's banking. At the time, money was "inelastic." In other words, only as much currency as was covered by its backing could be circulated. It may be asked whether the First Bank of the United States was really a central bank at all. Unlike a modern central bank, the First Bank of the United States did not set monetary policy, did not furnish an elastic currency, did not re-discount commercial piper, and did not act as a lender of last resort.

However, because it was one of the nation's largest corporations with branches spread across a large geographic area, it was able to conduct some functions similar to a central bank due to the sheer volume of its transactions.

The bank's notes were backed by substantial gold reserves which gave the country a stable national currency. By managing its lending policies and operations, the bank did alter the supply of money and credit which did, indirectly, affect the level of interest charged to customers. The bank would accumulate notes of the State banks and hold them in its vault. If it wanted to slow down growth, it would present the notes to the State banks for collection in gold. This would lessen the State bank's reserves, making it less able to lend. To increase growth, it would hold onto the notes, allowing the reserves in the State banks to build up, which made them more able to lend.

The charter for the First Bank of the United States was allowed to expire in 1811 and was not renewed. The next years saw a proliferation of federal bank notes necessary to finance the War of 1812. Five years elapsed between 1811 and 1816, when a second bank was considered.

The Second Bank of the United States 1816-1836

The War of 1812, with its naval blockade, impeded U.S. trade. This diminished the federal government's revenues as much of its revenue came from tariffs. By 1815, the U.S. was heavily in debt. Six men figured prominently in the establishment of a new, second, national bank, John Jacob Astor, David Parish, Stephen Girard, Jacob Barker, Alexander Dallas, and Representative John C. Calhoun.

The objective was to restore a stable currency, thereby avoiding bouts of inflation. President Madison, who originally opposed the creation of the First Bank of the United States, reluctantly admitted the need for another national bank to finance the war with Britain. But progress in the peace negotiations caused him to withdraw his support.

After peace was achieved in 1815, Congress rejected new efforts to create a second national bank. In the months that followed, however, the federal government's financial position deteriorated. Many State banks stopped redeeming their notes. This convinced Madison that it was necessary to move the country towards a more stable paper currency. The Second Bank of the United States was signed into law in 1816.

From the first two United States central banks, we learn that there are two reasons for a central banking system: (1) a more stable currency and (2) the ability to finance a war.

The second bank had a 20-year charter. It operated as a commercial bank accepting deposits and making loans to the public. Its Board consisted of 25 directors, five of whom were appointed by the President and confirmed by the Senate.

The capitalization of the Second Bank was $35 million, compared to $10 million for the First Bank. The Second Bank had 25 branches compared to 8 for the First Bank. The sheer number of branches aided the country's westward expansion.

Similarly to the First Bank, the Second Bank did not operate as a modern central bank. It did not set monetary policy, regulate other banks, or act as a lender of last resort. However, similar to the First Bank, its sheer size allowed it to conduct some rudimentary monetary policy setting. The Second Bank's notes were backed by substantial gold reserves giving the country an even more stable national currency. By managing its lending policies and operations, the Second Bank did alter the supply of money and credit in the general economy and did indirectly affect the interest rates charged to borrowers.

Similar to the First Bank, the Second Bank held notes of the State banks. If it wanted to slow growth, it could redeem notes for gold or silver which would reduce reserves for lending. If it wanted to increase growth, it could hold notes allowing the bank's reserves to accumulate, leaving the bank with greater reserves for lending.

In 1828, Andrew Jackson was elected President. In 1832, he was re-elected. A request to renew the bank's charter was sent to Congress in 1832, four years before its charter was due to expire. Though the request to renew passed both the House and the Senate, it did not have enough votes to overcome Jackson's veto.

President Jackson saw his 1832 election win as a validation of his anti-bank sentiment. Shortly after the election, he ordered that federal deposits be removed from the Second Bank and be put into State banks. The removal of federal deposits effectively put the Second Bank out of business. Both the First and Second Banks of the United States issued currency and acted, in some manner, on behalf of the United States Treasury. They both conducted normal banking operations including making commercial loans, accepting deposits, purchasing securities, and maintaining branches similar to a commercial bank. However, the government was required to purchase only 20 percent of the capital stock and appoint only 20 percent of the Board. This meant that 80 percent of the control of each bank remained in the hands of wealthy investors.

The large national banks, such as the First and Second Banks of the United States, were opposed by State banks which looked upon them as cartels compelling the common man to support them.

Andrew Jackson vetoed the legislation to renew the Second Bank of the United States which started a period of free banking. He took the position that every monopoly came at the expense of the public and took earnings away from the American people. Both banks, through their lending policies and flow of funds through their accounts, did alter the supply of money and credit in the general economy, which affected the interest rates charged to borrowers. But it appears as if their effect on interest was only a byproduct of their size rather than the realization of an objective.

Free Banking Period 1837-1862

The next period in the history of banking ran from 1837 to 1862 and was known as the Free Banking Period. During this period, only State chartered banks existed. They could only issue banknotes against gold and silver coin and their reserve requirements, interest rates for loans, and deposit and capital ratios were heavily regulated by the State in which they were located.

The Michigan Act of 1837 allowed State banks to become automatically chartered without first qualifying for operation with the State Legislature. This, unfortunately, increased the number of unstable banks. During this period, the real value of paper money was often less than its face value, and the financial strength of the issuing bank generally determined the size of the discount.

In 1797 there were 24 State banks. By 1837, there were 712. During the Free Banking Period, commercial banks had an average life expectancy of five years. About one-half of the banks failed, and about a third went out of business because they could not redeem their notes. During this period, some local banks tried to take over the function of a central bank and act to guarantee that certain bank notes would trade near par value, similar to a clearinghouse.

National Banking Act Period 1863-1907

The Civil War effectively removed the south's objections to centralized banking, as the south was no longer part of the Union. In 1863, as a means to help finance the Civil War, a system of national banks was created by the National Currency Act. Under it, each national bank had the power to issue standardized national bank notes backed by U.S. Treasury bonds.

In 1864, the National Currency Act was revised by the National Banking Act. In addition to providing loans for the Civil War, the National Banking Act created a system of national banks which were to have higher standards and more stringent reserve requirements than the State banks. It created the office of the Comptroller of the Currency, including its chief administrator, the Comptroller of the Currency.

The currency issued by the National Banking Act was known as the National Bank Note. All of the national banks were required to accept the notes of the other national banks at par value. National banks were required to secure their notes with U.S. Treasury bonds.

Here, we have our first introduction to the concept of "inelastic" currency. The National Banking Act's currency was considered inelastic because it was based on the fluctuating value of the U.S. Treasury bond. If the price of U.S. Treasury bonds fell, the national banks had to reduce the amount of currency they had in circulation. A National Bank Note could not expand beyond its backing and was considered, therefore, to be inelastic.

The Federal Reserve Act was not the first act to require that a bank maintain reserves. However, because the bank's currency was inelastic, if its reserves became drained, they could only be replenished by selling stocks and bonds, borrowing from a clearinghouse, or calling in loans. Its currency could not increase or decrease with the needs of business.

Because of the country's aversion to large banks, under the national banking system, few, if any, branches were allowed. As a result, each office operated as one-unit bank. Because of their small size, it became difficult for a one-unit bank to become large enough to operate efficiently or to diversify its loan portfolio. Further, because of the one-unit bank system, the reserves of the many banks became scattered around the country and could not be reached in time to replenish funds and avert a financial panic in a time of need.

Banks, being spread out around the country, created other problems. To clear checks and bank notes, banks would have to send an actual person to travel to the correspondent bank. This was an expensive endeavor, and to remedy this problem, clearinghouses were established.

Clearinghouses were private organizations created by banks to lower the cost of clearing checks and bank notes. Rather than having to physically send someone to other facilities, banks could send their representatives to clearinghouses in order to collect.

The success of cleaning house depended upon keeping the operations local. Banks in other cities had to form their own clearinghouses rather than clear their debts through New York.

Even though the National Banking Act required its banks to maintain reserves, its inelastic currency, few branches, scattered reserves, and the need for clearinghouses made the system fragile and ripe for a comprehensive reimagining. Further, at the time of the National Banking Act, farmers needed currency to bring their crops to market and to buy gifts for the holiday season. Under the National Banking Act, the inelastic currency could not respond quickly enough to the increased demand. As a result, the price of currency rose which caused interest rates to rise. Increased interest rates lowered the value of the bank's assets, making it more difficult to pay depositors.

Movement Towards Banking Reform 1863-1913

The conventional wisdom is that by the late 19th Century, bank depositors feared that their bank would run out of money. This caused them to withdraw their funds from their bank, effectively staging a "run" on the bank. It became necessary to find a way to cure the banks' liquidity problem so that depositors would not need to withdraw their funds. Between 1863 and 1913, there were five banking panics in New York and the nearby States alone.

There were three additional nationwide panics including the Panic of 1873, the Panic of 1893, and the Panic of 1907, making eight total bank panics. The Panic of 1873 appears to have been related to problems in the railroad business. The Panic of 1893 appears to have been related to gold reserves.

In 1895, J. P. Morgan assisted in rescuing America's gold standard when he headed a banking syndicate that loaned the federal government over $60 million dollars. The Panic of 1907 appears to have been related to traders attempting to corner the copper market. When they failed, the banks suffered bank runs which spread to affiliated banks. This led to the downfall of the Knickerbocker Trust Company, New York City's third largest trust. The collapse of the Knickerbocker Trust Company sent shock waves across the nation causing vast numbers of people to withdraw their funds from their banks.

Relative to the Panic of 1907, Mr. Morgan held a meeting of the country's top financial people at his home in New York.

He convinced them to bail out various faltering financial institutions in order to stabilize the markets. In light of this necessity, several people and progressive politicians feared a situation in which it would become periodically necessary for the government to ask rich people to bail out the country. It was feared that these rich people might garner too much power and become able to manipulate the country's financial system for their own gain.

In 1907, Paul Warburg, a partner in Kuhn, Loeb and Co., published an article in the New York Times calling for a modified central bank. In that same year, Jacob Schiff, the chief executive officer of the same firm, made a speech to the New York Chamber of Commerce stating that the country needed a central bank.

After the Panic of 1907, Republican Senator Nelson Aldrich and Republican Representative Edward Vreeland worked together on currency and banking reform. In 1908, Congress passed the Aldrich-Vreeland Act which provided for emergency currency and the establishment of the National Monetary Commission.

Senator Aldrich set up two commissions, one to study the American monetary system in depth and the other, headed by the Senator himself, to study the European central banking system.

Senator Aldrich took a trip to Europe to study its banking operations. When he embarked for Europe, he opposed central banking. However, when he saw the German banking system, he changed his mind. He thereafter believed that a central bank was better than the government issued bond system he previously supported.

By the fall of 1910, Senator Aldrich decided to convene a small group of people to consider how financial reform might be accomplished. This group included Senator Aldrich himself; Arthur Shelton, his private secretary; Henry Davidson; A. Piatt Andrew, an economics professor from Harvard who was the assistant Secretary of the Treasury;

Frank Van der Lip, President of National City Bank; and Paul Warburg. A member of the exclusive Jekyll Island Club located off the coast of Georgia arranged for the group to use the Club, perhaps the most exclusive Club in the world.

By the time of the Jekyll Island meeting, the problems with the banking system were well known. The group was concerned with financial panics which had disrupted economic activity periodically during the 19th Century. These panics triggered long and deep recessions.

As we have seen, some American banks had reserves. Due to the banking system, however, reserves were scattered throughout the country. During a crisis, the reserves could not be quickly accessed to supply cash when needed. Further, when banks had excess reserves, they were invested in call loans and stock, making them illiquid and difficult to use to supply cash.

In Europe, by contrast, bankers invested much of their portfolios in commercial paper which consisted of short-term loans to merchants and manufacturers. This commercial paper directly financed commerce and industry which provided banks with an asset which they could quickly convert to cash during a crisis.

The Jekyll Island participants also worried about the inelastic supply of currency in the United States. The value of the currency was linked to gold, and the quantity of currency available was linked to the supply of a special series of government bonds. The supply of currency neither expanded nor contracted with seasonal changes in demand causing interest rates to vary substantially from month to month.

Senator Aldrich knew that the Wall Street ties of his Jekyll Island group might arouse suspicion about their motives and could threaten the passage of a bill coming out of such a meeting. In light of this, he went to great lengths to keep the meeting a secret, adopting the ruse of a duck hunting trip.

Aldrich and his colleagues agreed on some broad principles – They wanted to establish a system in which there was an elastic currency supplied by a bank that held the reserves of all banks. It was understood that reserves alone would not cure the problem. The plan devised was to not only combine reserves from several member banks but to create an elastic currency which could expand and contract with the needs of business. This plan was brought to the forefront by two competing pieces of legislation: (1) the Aldrich Plan, and (2) the Federal Reserve Act.

By the end of their trip to Jekyll Island, Senator Aldrich and his colleagues developed a plan known as the Reserve Association of America. It would have 15 branches, each with a Board of Directors elected by its member banks. The branches would hold the reserves for the member banks, issue currency, discount commercial paper, transfer balances, and clear checks. The national body would set discount rates for the system and buy and sell securities.

Shortly after returning home, Senator Aldrich became ill and was unable to write the report for the group. Mr. Van der Lip and Mr. Strong traveled to Washington to put together a plan ready for presentation. The plan was presented to the **National Monetary Commission in January 1911.**

In the final report the name of the plan was changed from the Reserve Association of America to the National Reserve Association. It came to be commonly known as the Aldrich Plan, but the Aldrich name was removed for political reasons.

During the time leading up to the general election of 1912, Senator Aldrich and the people backing his plan, such as the people at Jekyll Island, were Republicans. Many Democrats opposed his plan on the theory that it would give the large banks and the private bankers too much influence over the country's financial system.

Though the Democrats opposed the Aldrich Plan, they did agree that a change was necessary. To this end, they put forth their competing plan, the Federal Reserve Act. Senator Robert M. La

Follette and Representative Charles Lindberg, Sr. maintained that the Aldrich Plan was a plan from Wall Street which favored the Money Trust. In response, Representative Arsene Pujo held a hearing within the House Banking Committee to investigate.

Neither Senator La Follette nor Representative Lindberg were called to testify. Even so, the Committee found that there was a Money Trust and that the New York bankers had a monopoly over the nation's money and credit. There was a concentration of money and credit in the hands of a relatively small number of men through their banking activities and interlocking directorates. The people guilty of such transgressions included J. P. Morgan, the Rothschilds, Kuhn, Loeb and Co., and others.

The bankers and the press concluded that the only way to break the monopoly was to enact banking and currency legislation such as the Federal Reserve Act which was being proposed to Congress. It was enacted one year later. The press demanded that the New York banking monopoly be broken by turning over the administration of the new banking system to the most knowledgeable banker of all, Paul Warburg.

Wilson won the election of 1912 largely because Theodore Roosevelt entered the race as a third-party candidate with his "Bull Moose Party." This allowed Wilson to defeat Taft. Wilson made William Jennings Bryant Secretary of State in consideration of his assistance with the election. In the election of 1912, the repudiation of the Aldrich Plan was made part of the Democrats' election platform. When Woodrow Wilson won the Presidency and the Democrats took control of both houses of Congress, the Aldrich Plan was shelved.

Even though the Aldrich Plan was not favored, the Democratic Party, including President Wilson himself, still wanted banking reform. In pursuance of that sentiment, the Chairmen of the House Committee on Banking and Currency, Carter Glass, and the Chairman of the Senate Committee on Banking and Currency, Robert Owen, introduced proposals to form a central bank based on draft legislation supported by Wilson. The Democrats demanded a reserve system and a currency supply owned by the government in order to counter the Money Trust.

The Aldrich Plan provided for one central bank, the National Reserve Association. It had 15 branches in the various locations. The branches would be controlled by the member banks. The National Reserve Association would issue currency backed by gold and commercial paper, and the currency would be the liability of the bank and not the government.

Bryant, representing the left wing of the Democratic Party, wanted a government owned central bank which could print paper money whenever Congress wished. He took the position that the Aldrich Plan gave the bankers too much power to print the government's currency.

President Wilson consulted a prominent lawyer, Louis Brandeis. He agreed with Mr. Bryant. However, President Wilson convinced both Mr. Brandeis and Mr. Bryant that his Federal Reserve system would be safe from Wall Street because (1) its currency, the Federal Reserve Note, would be made the obligation of the government; and (2) its Board, the Federal Reserve Board, would be appointed by the President and confirmed by the Senate and would act in Washington D.C. to oversee all of the banks in the system.

Among the alleged differences between the Aldrich Plan and the Federal Reserve Act, with the Aldrich Plan the bankers would issue the currency which would be the liability of the banks, whereas with the Federal Reserve Act, the government would issue the currency which would be the liability of the government.

With the Aldrich Plan, the bankers would appoint the Board which would oversee the banks, whereas with the Federal Reserve Act, the President would appoint the Board, with the advice and consent of the Senate.

Several Congressman including Owen, Lindbergh, La Follette, and Murdock claimed that the New York bankers feigned their disapproval of the Federal Reserve Act in hopes of persuading Congress to pass it, a reverse-psychology ploy. Ultimately, the Federal Reserve Act prevailed over the Aldrich Plan and was passed in December of 1913.

Chapter 3
The Federal Reserve

"I cannot morally blame all Americans for allowing, for instance, the birth of the Federal Reserve System and the money destruction that has followed. They are simply ignorant about it and don't know what happened or what is happening. They think that prices go up rather than that dollars go down."

                  Robert Prechter,
                  Financial Author

Operation of the Federal Reserve Act

As we learned, by the second half of the 19th Century, banks were beginning to experience liquidity problems. Depositors felt that the banks would not have enough money to repay their deposits. In 1895, it became necessary for J.P. Morgan to arrange a banking syndicate to loan $60 million dollars to the federal government to combat the banking crisis.

By the early 20th Century, the bankers began pushing for a central bank in the United States. In 1910, Senator Nelson Aldrich took a group to Jekyll Island. While there, they devised the Aldrich Plan. Another group, led by President Woodrow Wilson, devised a different plan, the Federal Reserve Act. Under the Aldrich Plan, the bankers would control a Board overseeing banking. Under the Federal Reserve Act, a government Board selected by the President with the advice and consent of the Senate would oversee banking. The Federal Reserve Act prevailed.

Under Article I, Section 8, of the United States Constitution, Congress has the legislative duty to issue money and regulate its value. For Congress to delegate this duty to an outside body, it would require an act of Congress. The Federal Reserve was created by an act of Congress. As it was created by an act of Congress, it could also be abolished by an act of Congress.

Prior to the Federal Reserve, banking was conducted under the National Banking Act. The currency under this act was known as a National Bank Note. A National Bank Note was considered inelastic because it could not be expanded or contracted for the needs of business and was backed by a finite number of government bonds.

Also, under the National Banking Act, banks tended to be one-unit establishments with few branches and with reserves scattered around the country.

In 1913, Congress passed the Federal Reserve Act. The Federal Reserve Act states in its Preamble that it is an Act to establish Federal Reserve banks, to create an elastic currency, and to allow the rediscounting of commercial paper.

As the National Bank Note was inelastic, the Federal Reserve created a new currency, the Federal Reserve Note, the first dollar bill. The Federal Reserve Note was an elastic currency with the Fed being able to expand its volume quickly to meet the needs of business.

As a single central bank was not favored generally in the United States, the Federal Reserve Act created 12 reserve districts with a Federal Reserve Bank in each district. Each of the 12 Reserve Banks acted as a central bank. In this way the Act provided for 12 central banks rather than one. With the Federal Reserve Act, all of the national banks and as many of the State banks wished could join the Federal Reserve. The joining banks would become known as member banks.

It is interesting to note that the Federal Reserve was created initially to provide emergency cash to the banks to prevent panic. As time went on, however, its role expanded significantly to include managing the economy for an entire nation through setting interest rates and other monetary policy tools.

Member banks, to maintain liquidity, could borrow from one another at the **fed funds rate**. If unable to borrow from another member bank due to credit problems, a member bank could borrow from the Reserve Bank at its **Discount Window**, at the **Discount Rate**. This made the Fed the **Lender of Last Resort**. As provided under the Act, the banks could pledge rediscounted paper as collateral.

The Discount Rate was slightly higher than the fed funds rate. Initially, each Reserve Bank set its own Discount Rate. Eventually, they would all agree to set the same rate. It has been stated that borrowing from the Discount Window implied that the borrowing bank was in financial trouble. Notwithstanding this, the Discount Window remains in use today and has been used as a significant tool during the 2008 financial crisis and the COVID-19 pandemic.

Initially, bank reserve requirements could be changed. When reserve requirements were lowered, there was more money to lend which reduced interest rates and stimulated the economy.

When reserve requirements were raised, there was less money to lend which would increase interest rates and cool the economy.

Today, changing a bank's reserve requirements is no longer one of the Fed's tools as in 2020 reserves were eliminated.

In the 1920s, after World War I, the Fed bought government securities to improve its earnings position. From this activity, it learned, some say by accident, which buying and selling securities would affect the broader economy.

Section 12A of the Federal Reserve Act created the Federal Open Market Committee (the "FOMC"). Section 14 grants to the Federal Reserve the authority to conduct Open Market Operations.

With **Open Market Operations**, the Fed prints money out of thin air and buys short-term securities from the bank. Rather than giving the cash to the bank, it injects the purchase price into the bank's reserves. This increases reserves which, in turn, lowers interest rates, increases the money supply, and stimulates the economy.

The Fed may constrict the economy by selling securities. When this is done, the Fed removes the purchase price from bank reserves. This decreases reserves which, in turn, raises interest rates and cools the economy. With respect to Open Market Operations, initially, the activity was disjointed with some banks conducting them, and others not. Eventually, the Banking Acts of 1933 and 1935 solidified Open Market Operations.

From 1920 until 1970, the Fed used Open Market Operations to manage the economy by managing reserves and short-term interest rates. However, in 1970, that changed.

In 1970, rather than using Open Market Operations, the Fed began to use the fed funds rate (or changes in the fed funds rate) to manage the economy. It would set a target range for the fed funds rate and use its tools to steer the rate to the target.

The Fed will set a target range below the existing rate to lower rates and stimulate the economy or set a target above the existing rate to increase rates and cool the economy.

It should be emphasized that the Fed does not set the fed funds rate itself. It only sets a target range for the fed funds rate.

At this point, the use of Open Market Operations became seen as an indirect method of managing the economy whereas setting a target range for the fed funds rate was seen as a more direct method.

From 1970 until 1979, the FOMC set a target range for the fed funds rate and used Open Market Operations to steer the fed funds rate to the target. In 1979, the newly appointed Fed Chairman, Paul Volcker, announced that rather than use the target for the fed funds rate, the Fed would instead use the money supply (non-borrowed reserves). This caused the fed funds rate to fluctuate wildly, driving interest rates to new highs.

In 1982, the Fed ended its short-lived experiment with targeting the money supply and returned to setting a target range for the fed funds rate.

From 1982 until the 2008 financial crisis, the Fed set a target range for the fed funds rate and used Open Market Operations to steer the fed funds rate to the target. With the 2008 financial crisis, the Fed reduced the fed funds rate to near zero. With the fed funds rate near zero, the Fed could no longer use the lowering of the fed funds rate as a way of stimulating the economy. The Fed resorted to Quantitative Easing.

With **Quantitative Easing**, the Fed would create money out of thin air and use it to make large-scale purchases of long-term securities, mortgage-backed securities, and other assets from the banks. Rather than give the cash to the banks, the Fed would give the bank a credit to its reserve account. This created an ample reserve environment. Congress allowed the Fed to pay interest on reserve balances kept by the banks at the central bank.

As we may see, since 1970, with the exception of 1979 to 1982, the Fed has managed the economy with the fed funds rate. It sets a target range for the fed funds rate and steers the fed funds rate to the target. The Fed has employed two methods of steering the fed funds rate. Before 2008, the Fed steered the fed funds rate to its target with Open Market Operations. After 2008, the fed steers the fed funds rate to its target with the interest on reserve balances.

Because the interest on reserve balances is an administered rate, a rate that may be set by the Fed itself, the Fed can steer the fed funds rate by adjusting a rate that it sets. **Presently, interest on reserve balances is the primary tool the Fed uses to adjust the fed funds rate.** The Fed uses the fed funds rate because it is the rate charged by one bank to another bank for overnight loans and as such influences several different interest rates in the economy.

The Federal Open Market Committee

THIS IS HOW THE FED MANAGES THE ECONOMY BY USE OF THE FED FUNDS RATE:

The Federal Open Market Committee (FOMC) meets 8 times a year to make monetary policy decisions. The meetings generally last two days and take place at the Fed's headquarters in Washington D.C. During these meetings, committee members review economic data, discuss monetary policy options, and make decisions on interest rates and money supply. At the end of each regular meeting, the FOMC releases a policy statement announcing its decision, including an assessment of the economy.

From the data, the FOMC will determine whether the economy needs to be stimulated or cooled. **If the economy needs stimulation, the FOMC will set a new target range for the fed funds rate below the existing rate.** This will lower the new fed funds rate and stimulate the economy. **If the economy needs cooling, the FOMC will set a new target range for the fed funds rate above the existing rate.** This will raise the fed funds rate and cool down the economy.

30 minutes after the FOMC decision is released, the Chairman of the Federal Reserve Board holds a press conference to explain the decision to the public. If the economy needed stimulation, the Fed Chairman will announce that the new fed funds rate will be lower than the existing rate by a certain number of basis points, typically 25 or 50 basis points. 25 basis points is ¼ of one percent. 50 basis points is ½ of one percent. If the economy needed cooling, the Fed Chairman will announce that the new fed funds rate will be higher than the existing rate, typically 25 or 50 basis points. He could also announce that there will be no change in the fed funds rate.

The fed funds rate is not a public interest rate. However, if the new fed funds rate is lower or higher than the existing rate, the FOMC presumes that public interest rates for such things a house, car, and credit cards will follow the direction of the new rate.

With Quantitative Easing, when the Fed adds a credit to the bank's reserves, the bank was supposed to lend those funds to stimulate the general economy and lower long-term interest rates. Problems arose when the banks, rather than lending the funds it receives, chooses to use the funds for their own purposes. Some banks might keep the funds in their reserve account, purchase other financial assets, pay down debt, buy their own stock, or shore up their balance sheets.

In defense of the banks, when QE came into existence, there was a lack of qualified borrowers. Also, the influence was indirect, as the money became a credit to bank reserves rather than a payment to individuals or businesses. QE did lower some long-term interest rates and did increase some mortgage originations.

When the QE programs ended after the Pandemic era, policy shifted from Quantitative Easing to Quantitative Tightening. Quantitative Tightening ended in late 2025, causing Fed policy to shift to a neutral stance, setting the stage for future easing.

Changes in the fed funds rate influence short-term interest rates, which, in turn, impacts a wide range of consumer and business borrowing costs such as car loans, credit cards, personal loans, and business loans.

However, longer-term rates, such as house loans, can be affected by broader market forces and may sometimes move independently of the Fed's direct policy changes.

Further, individual banks are not required to align their rates perfectly with the Fed's announcement and might adjust their rates based on their own assessment of market conditions. But generally, public interest rates will follow the direction that the fed funds rate has been taken.

In the approximately 112 years before the Fed, there were 6 depressions. However, the inflation rate was only .4 percent annually. In the same number of years after the Fed, there has been only one depression. But the inflation rate is 3.1 percent annually, on average. If we abandon the Fed, we may have more depressions but less inflation. If we keep the Fed, we may have fewer depressions but more

inflation, and this inflation may erode the buying power of the dollar, as we have seen.

If one were to abandon the Fed, please keep in mind that one of the most important functions of the Fed is to watch over the economy. The Fed watches the economy to determine whether it needs stimulation, such as during a recession, or cooling, such as during periods of high inflation.

If the Fed were abandoned, unless we are willing to put all of our trust in the banks, we will still need some entity to watch over the economy and make adjustments as necessary or suffer more setbacks while waiting for the market to correct itself. If the Fed is abandoned and a new entity is created to watch over the economy, such an entity might become part of the Treasury Department, in which case the control of the economy might move closer to the Executive Branch than one might wish.

If the Executive Branch took over the economy, it might do such things as lower the interest rates to win an election or improve the person's political image. The Fed, as it exists now, is an independent Board chosen with the advice and consent of the Senate. It might be more objective than the government employees working at Treasury at the behest of the President and Secretary of the Treasury.

Though the fed funds rate is not a public interest rate, it is presumed that if the Fed adjusts the fed funds rate, the public interest rates will follow in the same direction to either stimulate or cool the economy. Basically, the Fed, from its extensive financial data, determines whether the economy needs to be stimulated, such as during a recession, or cooled, such as during periods of high inflation. The Fed determines a target for the fed funds rate and either lowers it to stimulate the economy or raises it to cool the economy.

The Federal Reserve's Emergency Lending Power

As we have seen, the Fed's traditional method of operation was to create money out of thin air and use it to purchase securities. Instead of paying for the securities, it would add the purchase price to the bank's reserves. As the bank's reserves increased, interest rates would become smaller, which would stimulate the economy.

When this was done, the Fed would increase the reserve account of a financial institution rather than extend credit directly to individuals, partnerships, or corporations.

During the 2008 financial crisis and the COVID-19 pandemic, the Federal Reserve began extending credit to individuals, partnerships, or corporations directly.

From where did the Fed obtain the authority to do this?

Direct credit extensions were made under the authority of the Section 13(3) of the Federal Reserve Act added in 1932.

Rather than extending credit exclusively to financial institutions, under Section 13(3), the Fed may extend credit to individuals, partnerships, or corporations:
1. Under exigent circumstances.
2. When the notes, drafts, and bills of exchange are of a type that are eligible for discount by member banks.
3. When the notes, drafts, and bills of exchange are indorsed and otherwise secured to the satisfaction of the Federal reserve bank; and
4. When the individual, partnership, or corporation is unable to secure adequate credit accommodation from other banking institutions.

The Dodd-Frank Act of 2010 requires that the Fed seek approval from the Treasury Secretary to lend under Section

13(3). It also requires that such loans be made available to a broad class of borrowers rather than to just a single borrower. The emergency lending power added in 1932 was used for the 2008 financial crisis and the COVID-19 pandemic, which were found to present exigent circumstances.

As to the 2008 financial crisis, the program was used, but no funds were lent to single borrowers, an activity which was not prohibited until two years later by the Dodd-Frank Act of 2010. As to the COVID-19 pandemic, the program was used in 2020 when funding became unavailable on reasonable terms due to disruptions in the credit markets. The government maintains its power to appropriate funds for emergencies and may do so to cover the Fed for potential losses from the emergency loans.

THE FEDERAL RESERVE'S TIMELINE

1913 - 1920: THE FED ACTED AS THE LENDER OF LAST RESORT

1920 - 1970: THE FED MANAGED THE ECONOMY WITH OPEN MARKET OPERATIONS

1970 - PRESENT (EXCEPT 1979-1982): THE FED MANAGES THE ECONOMY WITH THE FED FUNDS RATE

1970 - 2008: THE FED STEERED THE FED FUNDS RATE TO ITS TARGET WITH OPEN MARKET OPERATIONS

2008 - PRESENT: THE FED STEERS THE FED FUNDS RATE TO ITS TARGET WITH INTEREST ON RESERVE BALANCES

A History of the Federal Reserve Prior to 2008

In the 1920s, under the leadership of Benjamin Strong, the Fed made its initial foray into conducting monetary policy.

Strong and other Fed officials discovered that when they engaged in the Open Market Operations of buying and selling securities, the general economy would respond.

To take advantage of this, in 1923, the Open Market Investment Committee was established with Strong as its chair. The Fed began to use Open Market Operations to proactively affect monetary policy.

In 1924 and 1927, the economy experienced recession. In response, the Fed made substantial open market purchases in both years. Open market purchases lowered interest rates which led to recovery.

In 1928, the Fed's focus turned towards the stock market. The Fed debated what steps it should take to ensure that Federal Reserve funds were not used to engage in stock market speculation.

In the late 1920s, the Fed sold securities and increased discount rates, two things which generally tighten the economy.

In 1929, the Federal Reserve Board issued new guidelines which prohibited banks from making stock market loans when borrowing from their Federal Reserve accounts. It cannot be ruled out that this economic tightening ended the economic expansion of the 1920s and contributed to the Great Depression. As a result of the Great Depression, Congress enacted the Banking Acts of 1933 and 1935.

In the wake of the stock market crash of 1929, commercial banks were sustaining losses from volatile equity markets. Under the Banking Act of 1933, commercial banks were no longer allowed to deal in securities, and investment banks were no longer allowed to have close connections with commercial banks.

The 1933 Act also created the Federal Deposit Insurance Corporation (FDIC), which insures bank deposits up to a set amount with money collected from the banks. The 1933 Act also created the Federal Open Market Committee (FOMC). The Federal Open Market Committee was then revised by the Banking Act of 1935.

The Banking Act of 1935 was divided into three Titles. Title II deals with Open Market Operations and the rearrangement of the power structure within the Federal Reserve System itself.

As we have seen, the first Open Market Operations were undertaken in the early 1920s under no particular organizational plan. Before 1922, it was found that Open Market Operations in one reserve district could affect markets in other reserve districts. In 1922, to enhance coordination, the Reserve Banks in New York, Boston, Chicago, Cleveland, and Philadelphia created an informal committee to conduct Open Market Operations.

In 1923, with the consent of the Federal Reserve Board, the informal committee became a formal committee called the Open Market Investment Committee (OMIC). The OMIC directed that a single account would be established to conduct Open Market Operations for the entire system. This was a voluntary arrangement.

The OMIC was replaced with the OMPC, still a voluntary arrangement. In 1933, due to economic conditions, several Reserve Banks refused to cooperate with the open market activities of the other banks. In response, the Banking Act of 1933 changed the OMPC, which was voluntary, to the Federal Open Market Committee (FOMC), which could make decisions that were binding on all of the banks.

The Banking Act of 1935 superseded this arrangement by creating the modern structure of the FOMC which was to include the seven Governors from the Board of Governors, the president of the New York Fed, and four additional bank presidents.

The FOMC directed Open Market Operations for the entire system. When the Banking Act of 1935 established the Federal Open Market Committee, the president of the New York Reserve Bank was made a perpetual member, with four of the other presidents rotating membership on the committee for a period of time.

Title II changed and expanded the balance of power within the Federal Reserve System. Power was shifted from the 12 Reserve Banks to the Federal Reserve Board located in Washington, DC.

The Fed continued with setting interest rates confirmed by traditional Open Market Operations as its primary work from the 1920s until the financial crisis of 2008. In 2008, it was required to transition to a different form of Open Market Operation. The following is a brief history of this progression.

Under the Banking Act of 1935, the Federal Reserve Board was renamed. It became the Board of Governors of the Federal Reserve System. The leader of the Board, who was previously called the governor, was renamed the Chairman. Today, the Board Chairman leads the Board in Washington in making monetary policy.

The Board became more independent of the executive branch. The Secretary of the Treasury and the Comptroller of the Currency were taken off of the Board.

The Board became divided into camps, the Board, which set reserve requirements and interest rates, and the FOMC, which handled Open Market Operations. The initial bill received much opposition. Opposition came from people who feared inflation and the centralization of monetary policy in Washington and those who opposed the Board setting reserve requirements and interest rates. The Federal Reserve's Open Market Committee implemented monetary policy by establishing the interest rate target it deemed necessary to drive the economy and then using Open Market Operations to keep it within the target range.

The fed funds market came into existence in the 1920s, with daily quotes first published in 1928. The Fed first published daily fed funds rates in 1954. Initially, the Fed used both the Discount Rate and the fed funds rate, but by the 1950s, fed funds rate was becoming primary.

By 1970, the Fed began to manage the economy by setting a target range for the fed funds rate and steering the fed funds rate to its target with Open Market Operations.

The Fed did this until the financial crisis in 2008 after which it abandoned the traditional Open Market Operations altogether in favor of the more super-charged operation known as Quantitative Easing.

After a poor performance during the Great Depression, from 1941 to 1945, the Fed supported World War II by maintaining low interest rates for government borrowing. After the War, the Fed grappled with postwar growth and inflation, adjusting interest rates and regulating the money supply to control inflation and allow growth.

In 1951, the Fed and Treasury reached the Treasury-Fed Accord of 1951 which established the Fed's greater independence in the management of the economy. In August 1971, during the Nixon Administration, the United States went off of the gold standard. The dollar became fiat currency, backed only by the full faith and credit of the United States and not backed by precious metals or securities.

Starting in the 1970s, the Fed began scheduling meetings to set and announce the fed funds rate. At this time, the Fed began to undertake its dual mandate of fostering price stability and full employment within an inflation range of 2 percent.

In the late 1970s, during the tenure of Paul Volcker, the interest rate reached as high as 20 percent. Mr. Volcker chose to fight inflation by expanding the money supply rather than by adjusting the fed funds rate. This went on from 1979 until

1982.

In 1982, the Fed returned to managing the economy by managing the fed funds rate, rather than by increasing the money supply. The Fed began to take on the role of inflation fighter and unemployment watchdog. It set a goal for inflation at 2 percent per year. In 1987, Alan Greenspan took over as Chairman where he would remain for 18 years.

From 2001 to 2005, the Fed was loose. It cut interest rates from over 6 percent to 1 percent. When housing prices soared, the Fed tightened by rapidly raising interest rates between 2005 and 2007. In 2006, Ben Bernanke took over as Chairman of the Fed. Soaring interest rates caused the financial system to collapse bringing about the 2008 financial crisis.

History of the Federal Reserve After 2008

Before the Federal Reserve, the United States experience several bank panics, including the Panic of 1792, 1819, 1837, 1857, 1873, 1884, 1893, 1896, and 1907. The banking system was inherently unstable due to a lack of a central bank, an inelastic money supply, and a shortage of emergency cash. The Federal Reserve addressed these problems by forming 12 central banks, creating an elastic currency not overly tied to gold, silver, or securities, and providing a method to get emergency cash to the banks.

To provide emergency cash, the Federal Reserve allowed member banks to borrow from one another and, if unable to do so, borrow from the Fed itself from the Discount Window where the Fed acted as the Lender of Last Resort, even allowing the banks to rediscount commercial paper.

As time went on, the Fed did not use its Lender of Last Resort function as much as it was originally thought that it might. After 1920, the Fed became more concerned with managing the economy.

After the Federal Reserve came into being, the economy suffered the Great Depression. One criticism of the Fed in that connection was that it did not perform its function as Lender of Last Resort as well as it might have.

The Lender of Last Resort function did, however, come back to the forefront during two severe economic crises experienced by the United States. These were the **2008 financial crisis** and the **COVID-19 pandemic crisis**. Before examining each of the crises individually, it might be interesting to note, in general terms, how they were handled.

With respect to both events, ultimately the Fed and the government worked together to achieve a resolution, with the Fed taking the lead with the 2008 financial crisis and the government taking the lead with the COVID-19 pandemic.

The 2008 Financial Crisis - TARP

The 2008 financial crisis was caused by a collapse of the U.S. housing bubble fueled by mortgage loans having been made to unqualified buyers and the bundling of those loans into securities sold in the securities markets.

When the home buyers defaulted, massive losses were sustained by lenders and institutions holding the bundled assets. In its capacity as Lender of Last Resort, before government involvement, the Fed was tasked with dealing with the crisis.

The Fed had extensive experience with printing money out of thin air and buying short-term securities from the bank to increase bank reserves, lower interest rates, and stimulate the general economy in a process known as Open Market Operations.

When funds were placed in bank reserves rather than being given directly to the people or businesses, the operation was deemed to be less inflationary. However, because of the severity of this particular crisis, buying short-term securities was deemed to be insufficient. A more super-charged operation was needed.

Since 1970, the Fed has used the targeting of the fed funds rate range as a method of managing the economy. However, when the Fed already reduced the fed funds rate to zero or near zero, it could no longer use the reduction of the fed funds rate as a way to stimulate the economy. When the Fed reduces the fed funds rate to zero or to near zero and the economy still requires stimulation, the Fed is left with Quantitative Easing.

With Quantitative Easing, the Fed prints money out of thin air in the form of electronic reserves and purchases long-term securities, mortgage-backed securities, and other assets from the bank. The funds become a credit to bank reserves.

This operation creates ample reserves, as opposed to limited reserves created by traditional Open Market Operations. The goal of Quantitative Easing is to flood the banking system with liquidity to lower long-term interest rates, encourage borrowing, and stimulate economic growth.

Quantitative Easing is considered to not be a bailout but merely a swap of assets for cash. Quantitative Easing is not the same as government spending which is funded by taxes or borrowing.

In general terms, the Fed's tools are designed to provide liquidity or short-term cash to maintain solvent institutions. However, its tools are not designed to provide capital to rescue insolvent ones. With the 2008 financial crisis, the major financial institutions were not just illiquid, but they were insolvent as they were holding trillions of dollars of toxic assets.

With the 2008 financial crisis, the Fed was able to provide some critical liquidity or cash. However, it lacked the authority under the Federal Reserve Act to inject capital directly into the banks to tackle the insolvency crisis.

The Fed made its best efforts to solve the 2008 financial crisis. However, based on the economic consensus, it is unlikely that the Fed could have solved such a crisis by itself without the cash injections from the government spending program known as the Troubled Asset Relief Program (TARP).

TARP provided the necessary legal avenue for the Department of the Treasure to inject capital directly into the banking system. TARP allowed banks to absorb losses and resume lending.

The government recovered most of the outlaid TARP funds through mandatory repayments, dividends, interest, and stock sales, ultimately resulting in a minimal net cost or slight profit.

Covid-19 Pandemic – The Cares Act

The onset of the corona virus disrupted employment and supply chains and triggered a financial crisis in March 2020, known as the COVID-19 pandemic. **Rather than using the Fed, the government intervened directly. In March 2020, Congress passed the Coronavirus Aid, Relief, and Economic Security Act (the CARES Act), a $2.2 trillion economic stimulus package aimed at providing rapid financial relief to individuals, businesses, and healthcare providers in response to the COVID-19 pandemic.**

Rather than credit bank reserves, the Act provided for direct stimulus checks, enhanced unemployment benefits, and paycheck protection paid directly to individuals and businesses. It also provided for loans and bailouts for distressed industries.

The Cares Act did, also, provide funding to the Treasury Department for the Fed to make emergency loans directly to individuals, businesses, and municipalities under Section 13(3) of the Federal Reserve Act. The Fed lengthened the term and lowered the rate at the Discount Window for depository institutions. The Fed kept interest rates low and conducted Quantitative Easing to support the government's operations.

TARP functioned largely as an emergency investment vehicle whereas CARES functioned more as a fiscal stimulus with limited repayment requirements, relying on economic recovery to normalize government revenue. Both TARP and CARES are part of the national debt. The entire $2.2 trillion of the CARES investment is part of the national debt. Though the initial TARP cash outlay was part of the national debt, because much of it was repaid with interest, the net impact on the national debt was only about $31 billion rather than the $700 billion authorized.

Returning to the Fed
And its Role in the 2008 Financial Crisis
And the COVID-19 Pandemic

The Fed conducted four rounds of Quantitative Easing with QE 1, 2, and 3 being conducted for the 2008 financial crisis and QE4 for the COVID-19 pandemic. The Fed further worked to support the government and its TARP cash injections by slashing interest rates and conducting Quantitative Easing. Quantitative Easing was designed to be, in theory, a temporary operation.

When the 2008 financial crisis passed, the Fed was supposed to sell the securities it was carrying on its balance sheet by utilizing an operation known as Quantitative Tightening (QT). This did not occur.

Janet Yellen took over the Chairmanship of the Fed from 2014 until 2018. In 2018, Jerome Powell became Fed Chairman.

In 2018, the Fed made a half-hearted effort to sell securities, but it did not last long. When the stock market crashed and the economy weakened, the Fed returned to Quantitative Easing. Then in 2020, before it could begin to pay for the Quantitative Easing that it had already conducted for the 2008 financial crisis, the COVID-19 pandemic came to fruition.

Rather than paying for the Quantitative Easing it had already conducted, it became necessary for the Fed to launch a new, massive Quantitative Easing program known as QE4. The Fed, not wanting to make it more difficult to find work, waited a long time before raising interest rates again. The Fed waited until 2022 to do so. Between 2020 and 2022, the annual inflation rate reached 6.34 percent. To fight inflation, the Fed increased interest rates 11 times between 2022 and 2023. By 2023, inflation began to fall.

The Fed's last rate hike of 25 basis points took place in July 2023. As of January 2024, the fed funds rate was 5.4 percent, the highest since 2002. In September 2024, the Fed cut the fed funds rate by 50 basis points (one-half of one percent), just 45 days prior to an election. TARP closed on September 30, 2023. The World Health Organization declared that the pandemic phase of COVID-19 was over May 5, 2023.

Did Quantitative Easing Work

Quantitative Easing achieved some of its goals but missed others. QE removed toxic subprime mortgages kept interest rates low enough to revive the housing market. Quantitative Easing did stimulate some economic growth, but it did not stimulate as much growth as the Fed hoped.

As was customary with the Fed, then funds were given to the bank to be placed in bank reserves. When this occurred, rather than lending out the money which would have stimulated growth, the banks kept some of the money which they used to pay dividends and make stock buybacks. This tripled the banks' stock prices but did not help ordinary citizens. QE did not cause the widespread inflation that was anticipated. But it did lead to asset bubbles, a situation in which an asset's price would increase without a corresponding increase in value. QE also raised the price of financial assets which contributed to an inequality in purchasing power.

Arguments Concerning the Initial Passage of
The Federal Reserve Act

The Federal Reserve System has now been in operation for over 100 years. With that much experience, one would think that its strong points and shortfalls would have been on display openly and would be well known by this time. We have a country which transitioned from independent storekeepers to mega-corporations in about 50 years which put tremendous pressure on the banking system by the early 20th Century.

As a nation of independent storekeepers, the government was asked to stay out of business. Business owners made a somewhat better living than the people working for them, but the differences were not significant. When businesses became very large and the number of unskilled and semiskilled workers increased, the workers had less input, leaving business owners the opportunity to reap great fortunes. The bargaining positions were no longer anywhere near equal.

Initially, big business tried to engineer success in the old fashion way, through hard work and competition. When that became too difficult (or too inconvenient), business owners resorted to monopolizing their respective industries. As monopolies became illegal by 1890 with the Sherman Antitrust Act, monopolization required the government to establish regulatory commissions. The regulatory commissions could then be taken over by the allies of big business, and competition could be eliminated in the name of opposing monopoly.

Speaking on the same day that the Federal Reserve Act was passed, Representative Charles A. Lindbergh, Sr. (the father of the famous aviator whose child was kidnapped), stated the following: "This is the Aldrich bill in disguise, the difference being that by this bill the Government issues the money, whereas by the Aldrich bill the issue was controlled by the bank … Wall Street will control the money as easily through this bill as they have heretofore."

The Reserve Banks were owned by commercial banks which were owned by their stockholders. Reserve Banks would continue to be run by the same people, even while they were being overseen by a government Board. It appears as if the New York Reserve Bank would become the actual central bank. In this way, its stockholders would become the actual owners of the Federal Reserve.

Ferdinand Lund in his book pointed out, "In practice, the

Federal Reserve Bank of New York became the fountainhead of the system of twelve regional banks, for New York was the money market of the nation. The other eleven banks were so many expensive mausoleums erected to salve the local pride and quell the Jacksonian fears of the hinterland."

Were the bankers acting for a profit motive? I do not believe that anyone reading these words would disagree with the proposition that if one knew today what the interest rate would be tomorrow, he could reap great profits.

However, we have very little anecdotal evidence that this occurred. We have only statements made at the time of the passing of the Act to the effect that by virtue of the Act (1) the President would become the absolute dictator of all finances, (2) the bankers would have the power to inflate or deflate the currency, (3) loans could be granted or called in for the purpose of influencing the price of securities, or (4) customers could be refused credit if they opposed the political views of their bank.

There is some evidence that Presidents have tried to persuade the Fed to lower interest rates to affect their re-election bids but sweeping assertions that the Fed acted improperly have not been reported or, at least, not reported very well, though presently the President appears to be pressuring the Board Chairman to lower rates. It is interesting to note that the two highest ranking government supporters of the Federal Reserve Act, shortly after its passage, changed their minds.

William Jennings Bryan, the then Secretary of State, wrote:

> **"That is the one thing in my public career that I regret – my work to secure the enactment of the Federal Reserve Law."**

In 1916, just three years after the law's enactment, President Woodrow Wilson stated:

"I am a most unhappy man. I have unwittingly ruined my country. A great industrial nation is controlled by its system of credit. Our system of credit is concentrated. The growth of the nation, therefore, and all of our activities are in the hands of a few men. We have come to be one of the worst ruled, one of the most completely controlled and dominated Government in the civilized world – no longer a Government by free opinion, no longer a Government by conviction and the vote of the majority, but a Government by the opinion and duress of a small group of dominant men."

In theory, the Federal Reserve is non-political. Politicians are supposed to be unable to sway the operation of the Federal Reserve. This was one of the main points that President Wilson used to secure the passage of the Act. Presently, however, the Fed lowered the interest rate by 50 basis points, which is substantial, 45 days before the national election in 2024.

Theories in Favor of the Act

On the plus side of the ledger, the Fed acts as a clearinghouse for banks, helping banks settle interbank payments. Though this service may be provided by traditional banks, there is a percentage of time during which a traditional bank cannot conduct clearinghouse services, which is usually during bank panics, when such services are needed.

During a financial panic, bank clearinghouses will generally fail. Prior to the Fed, there were numerous instances when recessions turned into depressions because of such failures.

Also, on the plus side, the Fed has always maintained that it is not funded by the taxpayers. Instead, the Fed receives its funding from the interest it receives on the securities it purchases through open-market operations and from interest on loans to banks and other fees such as fees for clearing checks and transferring funds. Then, after paying the operating expenses, the Fed does not keep its profit but returns any profits it to the Treasury.

The duty to regulate the value of money is an express power of Congress set forth in Article I, Section 8 of the United States Constitution. With the Federal Reserve Act, Congress has delegated this duty to the Federal Reserve.

While Congress has the power to delegate duties, it does not have the power to abdicate itself from its responsibility to oversee those duties. As we know, the Federal Reserve Act created 12 reserve districts, each with a Reserve bank as well as member banks which contribute their reserves. Under the Act, member banks may borrow from one another at the fed funds rate and, if unable to do so due to credit problems, may borrow from the Fed at the Discount Window, at a slightly higher rate, making the Fed the Lender of Last Resort.

The Fed continues to be engaged in this lending endeavor. However, after World War I, after buying and selling bonds to support the War effort, it decided to also engage in managing monetary policy; something for which there is no provision in the Act.

To do this, the Fed began using open-market operations to both influence the interest rate and increase the money supply. The Fed would add the money created by its Open Market Operations to the bank reserves rather than pay individuals and businesses directly, except under the terms of its emergency lending powers codified in Section 13(3) of the Act.

Both prior to the passage of the Act and 100 years later, members of Congress continue to opine that the Fed, with its Open Market Operations and Quantitative Easing, added so much money to the economy that inflation was the obvious byproduct and that this inflation worked to the benefit of the wealthy and big banks and to the detriment of the poor and middle class.

However, the Fed has used its tools to fight off over 20 recessions as well as the economic calamities brought about by the 2008 financial crisis and the COVID-19 pandemic. I believe that one could make a strong case that over the years people suffered losses due to inflation. However, if the Fed had not acted, there might have been even more economic downturns, and they might have been serious.

Theories in Opposition to the Act

From a strict legal standpoint, abolishing the Fed would be fairly easy. The Fed was established by an Act of Congress, and it appears as if it may be abolished by another Act of Congress, even though the McFadden Act of 1927 re-chartered the Federal Reserve Act and provided that it would exist in perpetuity.

When Andrew Jackson ended the Second Bank of the United States, he simply pulled the accounts, allowed the Second Bank to be taxed by the federal and State governments, terminated the authority of the Second Bank to regulate other banks, and ended the ability of the Second Bank to establish reserves.

Perhaps the most serious recent effort to abolish the Fed has come from Senator Mike Lee and Representative Thomas Massie. In 2024, they introduced a bill to repeal the Federal Reserve. The country would thereafter most likely return to traditional banking.

The reason for the bill given by Representative Massie was that "Americans are suffering under crippling inflation, and the Federal Reserve is to blame."

Even in 1913, before the provisions of the Act were put into effect, just from its text, certain politicians and writers felt that the Act could lead to economic problems.

When testifying before the Senate committee, Alfred Crozier stated:

"Both measures rob the government and the people of all effective control over the public's money, and vest in banks exclusively the dangerous power to make money among the people scarce or plenty."

As we may see, on the basis of the text of the Act alone, some were convinced that the banks would have too much power to inflate the money supply. For those people, it would not take 100 years of living under the Act to understand that it gave the banks too much power.

The Fed has been criticized for its lack of transparency as the people running it are not elected, that it controls the money supply and may pump trillions of dollars into the economy, and that it is unable to live up to its self-proclaimed dual mandate of producing stable prices and low unemployment.

The Fed does have unelected officials. This was done to separate its operation from the control of the government. The Fed does pump much money into the economy, but this is done, it maintains, to control the risk of the economy worsening.

As to its ability to produce stable prices and low unemployment, these are truly daunting tasks. The most prolific stock traders often underperform the market.

Managing an economy as large and diverse as the United States is nearly impossible, and the markets take a long time to correct which may cause many to suffer while a correction is taking place. The Fed devalues the dollar which has lost 96 percent of its purchasing power since 1913. It increased the money supply over 1,100-fold between 1913 and 2006.

Representatives Ron Paul and Thomas Massie look at the Federal Reserve Act from an egalitarian standpoint. They maintain that the Federal Reserve helps the big banks and the wealthy at the expense of the poor and middle class.

> **"What's happening is there's transfer of wealth from the poor and middle class to the wealthy. This comes about because of the monetary system we have. When you inflate a currency …, the middle class get wiped out, so the people who get to use the money first, which is created by the Federal Reserve System, benefit, so the money gravitates to the banks and to Wall Street. That's why you have more billionaires than ever before."**
>
> Ron Paul,
> **Member, United States House of Representatives**

"Monetizing debt is a closely coordinated effort between the White House, the Federal Reserve, the Treasury Department, Congress, the Big Banks, and Wall Street."

"Through this process, retirees see their savings evaporate due to the actions of a central bank pursuing inflationary policies that benefit the wealthy and connected. If we really want to reduce inflation, the most effective policy is to end the Federal Reserve."

Thomas Massie,
Member, United States House of Representatives

Characteristics of the Fed

There are approximately 4,614 banks. Approximately 35 percent are member banks of the Federal Reserve System. The rest are non-members. All nationally chartered banks must become member banks of the Reserve bank in their reserve district. State chartered banks may remain non-members. The number of banks has decreased from approximately 14,000 in 1988, to 10,000 in 1995, to 8,300 in 2000; and to 4,136 in 2022.

All member banks are required to hold reserves in their vaults or to deposit them with their Reserve bank. They are entitled to the services provided to member banks such as the use of the Discount Window.

The Fed's income comes from interest payments it receives from government securities that it owns as a result of its open market operations. The Fed does make a profit, but after paying its operational expenses, it turns its profits over to the

Treasury Department. An independent accounting firm audits both the Board and the Federal Reserve Banks. Certain aspects of the Fed mirror private companies; however, the Fed was created to serve the public. The Fed takes the position that the moves that it makes to help Wall Street are actually made to protect the public and not to benefit anyone in particular.

Even the Fed cannot prevent recessions, though by moving in the wrong direction, it can make them deeper. It has been contended that the moves it made to tighten may have pushed the economy from recession to depression during the Great Depression. Since the Great Depression, the Fed has only acted to inflate the economy. We cannot rule out the possibility that behind the scenes moves have been made to inflate or deflate the currency to achieve buying or selling opportunities, though they might not have been reported that way, or reported at all.

Since the conclusion of the First World War, the Fed has undertaken the task of setting monetary policy. Some argue that its actions have been either (1) too expansive, leading to inflation and the depreciation of the dollar, or (2) too tight, leading to unemployment and depression.

As the Fed may move interest rates high or low, it has the ability to either hinder or foster growth. Many Americans give too much credit or place too much blame on the President relative to the performance of the economy. A President does not have as much control over the economy as the Fed.

The Federal Reserve established a national currency and made it valid throughout the country. The Fed offers a rule-based monetary policy which leads to predictability. This policy helps the Fed explain its actions and allows the public to predict its movements.

For example, people understand that low interest rates will probably benefit business. The Fed conducts monetary policy to favor full employment and stable prices. The Fed regulates and supervises banks to ensure a sound financial system and the protection of consumer rights.

Without the Fed, the financial system would be run by banks. The Fed requires banks to undergo internal and external audits. Without the Fed, all audits would be internal, which could lead to corruption.

In my opinion, it is fairly safe to say that the Fed's action in increasing the money supply has led to inflation. In 1913, the money supply was 19.31 billion. By 1920, it doubled to 39.83 billion. By 1929, it reached 55.20 billion. By 1947, it was 166.76 billion. In 2006, it stopped reporting when the money supply passed 10 trillion, an 1,100-fold increase since 1913. Inflation rose relatively steadily throughout this period.

As difficult as it may be to believe, the Fed declines to take responsibility for high inflation. Over the past 2 years, the Fed has added nearly 5 trillion to the money supply, and prices have risen faster than they have in the past 40 years. Over the past 18 months, the money supply has increased 19 percent. Even with these figures available, the Fed blames inflation on disruptions in the supply chain or corporate greed. Contrary to those arguments we have the following:

> **"So: if the chronic inflation undergone by Americans, and in almost every other country, is caused by the continuing creation of new money, and if in each country its governmental 'Central Bank' (in the United States, the Federal Reserve) is the sole monopoly source and creator of all money, who then is responsible for the blight of inflation? Who except the very institution that is solely empowered to create money, that is, the Fed (and the Bank of England, and the Bank of Italy, and other central banks) itself?"**
>
> **Murray Rothbard,
> American Economist**

Who Owns the Federal Reserve

Though oversight under the Aldrich Plan was to be a Board of bankers whereas oversight under the Federal Reserve System became a government Board, at the Act's inception, the ultimate power under either plan rested with the individual regional Federal Reserve banks.

So, the question becomes: Who owns the individual regional Federal Reserve banks?

The stock in the original 12 regional Federal Reserve banks was purchased by national and State banks in their district. Because the Federal Reserve bank in New York set interest rates and directed open market operations, the stockholders of the New York bank should be considered the real directors of the entire system. The Federal Reserve Bank of New York issued 203,053 shares. Rockefeller and Kuhn, Loeb took 30,000 shares, making it the largest shareholder. J.P. Morgan's First National Bank took 15,000 shares. When they merged in 1955, they owned nearly 25 percent of the shares of the Federal Reserve Bank of New York. They could name anyone they wished, at any time they wished, to be Chairman of the Federal Reserve Board.

The Chase National Bank took 6,000 shares. Marine Midland took 6,000 shares. National Bank of Commerce of New York City took 21,000 shares.

It has been argued that the shareholders of these banks which own the stock of the Federal Reserve Bank of New York are the people who have controlled the political and economic destinies of the United States since 1914. They are the Rothschilds, Lazard Freres, Kuhn, Loeb, M.M Warburg Company, Lehman Brothers, Goldman Sachs, the Rockefeller family, and the J.P. Morgan companies.

Many argue that the developments following the passage of the Federal Reserve Act proved every allegation made by Thomas Jefferson in 1791, when he argued vehemently against a central bank. These allegations included the following: (1) that the subscribers to the Federal Reserve Bank stock had formed a corporation whose stock would be held by aliens; (2) that this stock could be passed down through a line of succession; (3) that this stock could not be made subject to forfeiture and escheat; (4) that the stock owners would receive a banking monopoly in violation of the laws against monopoly; and (5) that the stock owners would have the power to make laws paramount to the laws of the States.

Paul Warburg, perhaps the primary advocate for a central bank, retired from Kuhn, Loeb in order to serve on the Federal Reserve Board; however, he did not resign from several other Boards including Wells Fargo, Westinghouse, American Surety Company, and the Baltimore and Ohio Railroad.

Colonel House noted that he and Mr. Wilson knew that by passing the Federal Reserve Act they had created an instrument more powerful than the Supreme Court. In 1911, the Colonel completed a novel entitled Philip Dru, Administrator. Though fiction, the novel outlined a detailed plan for the future of government in the United States.

In response, certain Congressmen had a different philosophy:

> **"In a democracy the responsibility for the Government's economic policies, which so affect the economy, normally rest with the elected representatives of the people: in our case, with the President and the Congress. If these two follow economic policies inimical to the general welfare, they are accountable to the people for their actions on election day. With Federal Reserve independence, however, a body of men exist who control one of the most powerful levers moving the economy and who are responsible to no one."**
>
> **Wright Patman,**
> **Member, United States House of Representatives**

In 2009, Representative Ron Paul wrote a book entitled *End the Fed*. In it, he advocates abolishing the Federal Reserve System because it is immoral and unconstitutional and promotes bad economics. The book argues that the boom-and-bust cycles of business are caused by the Fed's actions.

In response to the 2008 financial crisis, in January 2024, Senator Rand Paul introduced the Federal Reserve Transparency Act. The bill calls for tougher audits of the Federal Reserve by the Governmental Accountability Office (GAO), a watchdog agency for Congress, to scrutinize the Fed's monetary policy.

In May 2024, Representative Thomas Massie introduced a bill known as H.R. 8421, the Federal Reserve Board Abolition Act. The bill calls for abolishing the Federal Reserve Board, abolishing the Federal Reserve Banks, and the repeal of the Federal Reserve Act altogether.

In the Senate, the bill was supported by Senator Mike Lee. Legislation to abolish the Fed has been opposed by the White House and the Federal Reserve. The Federal Reserve Chairman Janet Yellen wrote to Senators that such legislation would (1) undermine the independence of the Fed, and (2) likely lead to inflation fears and the fear of market rate interest.

I would submit that more careful scrutiny of the Fed's money creating operation might help to lessen the fear of inflation. At least people would know that the possibility that the Fed could cause inflation was receiving legitimate consideration.

Additionally, why would setting interest rates (the method used by the Fed) be favored over market interest rates (rates achieved through normal commercial activity) in a theoretically free market economy?

Supporters of the bill also state that the Fed has kept interest rates artificially low for decades, punishing savers in favor of businesses that use borrowed cash to fuel their operations. Representative Ron Paul states, "The Federal Reserve has the ability to create new money and spend it on whatever financial assets it wants, whenever it wants, while giving new money to whichever banks it wants."

Senator Rand Paul stated, "Low-income workers do not get the luxury of receiving the Fed's newly created money first, nor do they have the luxury of receiving near-zero interest rates that the wealthy do."

In support of maintaining the Federal Reserve as it is, the following has been the official policy statement of the Administration,

"Subjecting the Federal Reserve's exercise of monetary authority to audits based on political whims of members of Congress ... threatens one of the central pillars of the nation's financial system ..."

Whoever wrote this policy statement might wish to take another look at the Constitution. The power to regulate the value of money is given to Congress. The Federal Reserve exists only because it was created by Congress, and it only has the powers which were given to it by Congress. In short, Congress has greater authority over the financial system than the Fed and, with such, it should be free to audit the Fed whenever it wishes.

In support of H.R. 8421, Representative Massie stated the following:

"Americans are suffering under crippling inflation, and the Federal Reserve is to blame."

"During COVID, the Federal Reserve created trillions of dollars out of thin air and loaned it to the Treasury Department to enable unprecedented deficit spending."

Philosophically, I agree with Representative Ron Paul, Senator Rand Paul, Senator Lee, and Representative Massie that the Fed works for the rich and not for the vast majority of American citizens.

Senator Pat Toomey stated the case as follows:

> "This Fed policy has been pretty good for stocks – stock prices have gone up generally. It's been terrible for people with a bank-account."

After the 2008 financial crisis and the COVID-19 pandemic, through Quantitative Easing, the Fed injected a massive amount of money into the economy. Recently, an interest rate strategy was undertaken by the Fed under which if interest rates rise, there could be a loss of approximately $1.6 trillion, and this loss could become the debt of the taxpayers.

If such losses are possible, a comprehensive audit should be conducted. Through such an audit, we may learn whether the Fed is capable of providing all of the services that it is tasked to provide or whether it needs help to do so.

Also, it would seem that the people should have the right to know which banks receive the new money and how it is spent. Is the money spent to everyone's advantage or just to the advantage of a few rich people?

If a comprehensive audit shows that the Fed has been less than forthcoming about how it spends the people's money, perhaps abolishing the Fed may be something to consider.

I submit that a comprehensive audit is worth the expense and may provide information to which the people are entitled.

The argument that the specter of a comprehensive audit would "likely lead to an increase in inflation fears" is the precise opposite of reality. In reality, nearly everyone knows that the Federal Reserve has, at very least, contributed to inflation. From 1913 to 2006, it increased the money supply 1,100 times. In short, even if one agrees with everything that the Fed has done, it would be difficult to maintain that its stewardship has not contributed at least somewhat to inflation.

I believe that if people were told that an independent

organization was planning to comprehensively audit the Fed, they would be happy to hear that efforts were being made to find out why the Fed has been so instrumental in inflating the currency and what steps may be taken to correct that problem, if it is a problem at all.

Rather than opposing an audit, the people would, I believe, greatly favor one. I believe that the people would also be interested in knowing how the banks which receive the newly created money are chosen. The people are not given the new money created by the Fed; only favored banks receive this money.

Also, the people do not receive the low interest rates received by the rich. They receive only the interest rates that their vendors dictate after they are apprised of the changes in the fed funds rate.

We need a comprehensive audit of the Fed, and if there are irregularities or if it can be shown that the system operates for its own interest and not the interest of the people, a decision should be made whether the Fed should be abolished.

The fact that many oppose the idea of a comprehensive audit of the Fed shows that they might fear that such an audit could very well lead to a public outcry to abolish the Fed or, at least, to drastically amend it.

Those opposing a comprehensive audit contend that such an audit would increase inflation fears and the fear of market interest rates. From decades of operation, it is fairly clear that inflation has grown because of the policies of the Fed.

BEFORE THE FED, THE INFLATION RATE IN THE U.S. WAS .4 PERCENT PER YEAR; AFTER THE FED, IT HAS AVERAGED 3.1 PERCENT PER YEAR.

Non-Fed Banking

If the Fed is abolished, it will become necessary to find a successor banking operation so that people will continue to have a place to deposit their money and pay their bills. Several alternatives have been suggested over the years.

100 Percent Reserve Banks - For years, the Federal Reserve was a system of fractional reserves, that is, less than 100 percent of the depositors' money is required to be held in reserve. Loans above the reserve amount have been allowed, which creates new money.

As an alternative, a 100 percent reserve system could be put in place. With it, banks could accept deposits, and those deposits would be effectively warehoused. The bank could no loan more than it held in reserve. The bank's income would be derived from service charges for such things as arranging transfers of funds, clearing checks, etc.

Money would be considered a public utility. Why should the public pay interest to a banker to provide a medium of exchange that the government can provide at little or no cost? It is unlikely that this situation will be acceptable to the banking industry.

Gold Standard - As we know, in 1971 President Nixon took the country off of the gold standard. Money was no longer backed by gold. Backing by gold was a way to limit the amount of currency which could be printed during a particular time period, as currency could not be printed without the gold backing. This would limit inflation as fewer dollars would be allowed into circulation.

It is possible that if the banking business is returned to traditional banking rather than to the Federal Reserve, the new banks might wish to reestablish the gold standard. Though it is possible that prices will become depressed as there would be fewer dollars allowed into circulation, there might be less inflation. The Administration in Washington has spoken of abolishing the Fed and returning to the gold standard.

Printing Money - Some writers have advocated printing (creating) enough money to cover the nation's outstanding debt and use it to pay that debt. Thereafter, the country would engage in traditional banking with backed money.

Existing Non-Fed Banks - It would be quite simple to evaluate how well the Fed has performed over the years. Around 35 percent of banks are part of the Federal Reserve System. It would be relatively simple to compare the strengths and weaknesses of the Federal Reserve banks to the strengths and weaknesses of non-Federal Reserve banks.

Once compared, one may see how the non-Fed banks have fared in relation to the banks in the Federal Reserve system.

Traditional Banking - It is more likely that if the Fed were abolished, the U.S. would return to traditional banking. A traditional bank collects deposits, pays interest to depositors, charges interest to borrowers, and charges for peripheral financial services. By lending more that it has in reserve, it can increase money supply in some fashion, but not as quickly as a central bank.

Base vs. Book Money

A central bank, such as the Fed, creates what is known as **base money**, which consists of physical cash and digital reserves. Though commercial banks create most of the money supply, they do not create base money. They only create **book money** by making loans. With a commercial bank, when one gets a loan, the bank does not give cash to the borrower but creates a new deposit into the borrower's account, simultaneously creating a loan. This essentially creates new money for the borrower's ledger.

The central bank creates the ultimate form of money, cash and reserves, while commercial banks create claims on that money, that is, bank deposits, which it creates by lending.

Central banks, such as the Federal Reserve, have the unique power to create new cash and digital reserves that commercial banks hold in a process known as Direct Creation. If the Fed were abolished, money creation would shift to other entities such as the Treasury Department, private banks, commodities, or crypto currency, with Treasury potentially managing clearinghouses. This would create challenges such as a loss of central monetary control.

A private or government-run clearinghouse would be needed to settle interbank payments to replace a function now done by the Fed. Without a central authority to manage the money supply, the economy could swing wildly between inflation and deflation. If Treasury managed money, it could become highly politicized, unlike the Fed's relative independence.

Managing the Economy

If the Fed were abolished, though money creation might be a problem, perhaps a greater problem would be the management of the economy itself. One of the primary benefits of the Federal Reserve is providing a board or oversight committee which watches out for economic downturns or high inflation and then acts to correct them.

If we wish to maintain an oversight committee to watch the economy and act to stimulate it when needed, such as during 20 recessions, the 2008 financial crisis, and the COVID-19 pandemic, a committee will have to be constituted, either by private individuals or the government, to perform that function. This committee will need to be given the legal authority to do that which is already done by the Federal Reserve.

If such a committee is not established, during recessions or calamities such as the 2008 financial crisis or the COVID-19 pandemic, the people will have to wait for the markets to correct themselves before they may obtain financial relief, which might lead to years of very hard times.

If such a committee were established, the system would function similarly to the Federal Reserve but might require a governmental apparatus and a government payroll which means that the taxpayer may be involved with paying for this service.

Also, if such a committee were established, it would probably come under the auspices of the Department of the Treasury, which would bring it even closer to the executive branch than it is now, which is something that the Fed has tried very hard to avoid throughout its existence.

If oversight is left to politicians, it cannot be ruled out that they might, for example, move to lower interest rates to assist in a re-election campaign, including the campaign for President.

Further, without the Fed, there is no reason to believe that the new traditional banking system would do any better than the banks did before the Fed. During the first half of the 19th Century, when business was relatively simple, banks would still run out of money during certain times of the year, such as when crops needed harvesting or the holiday season called for gift giving.

If businesses as unsophisticated as these could develop a need for cash, it stands to reason that the larger businesses which came about in the second half of the century might have even a greater need for cash. **The fear that banks would lack sufficient cash to repay depositors led to the enactment of the Federal Reserve in the first place.** Does it not stand to reason that presently, in the 21st Century, the same need for cash would still exist? In the approximately 123 years before the passage of the Federal Reserve Act, the economy suffered 44 recessions and 6 depressions and depended upon the market turning around on its own for the country to return to normal.

One of the principal criticisms of the Fed has been that since the Great Depression, it has only acted to expand the economy. It has been reasoned that this has been responsible for inflation and has affected the poor and middle class more severely than the wealthy.

However, the Federal Reserve Act gives us an institution which is independent of the President and Congress and which watches over the economy and inflates it during recessions.

As we have seen, the Fed worked closely with the government to bring the economy out of the 2008 financial crisis and the COVID-19 pandemic. If this had not been done, we might have suffered a depression greater than the Great Depression.

Further, any of the other over 20 recessions which were smoothed over by the Fed might have blossomed into depressions.

I do not disagree with Representative Paul. The Federal Reserve, as it is now constituted, does favor the wealthy. New money will be given to the favored banks. The middle class will not see the benefit of low interest but will be saddled with market rate interest.

However, if we abolish the Fed and need an oversight committee to smooth over recessions, we will be in approximately the same position as we have been in with the Fed, but with the potential of greater taxpayer involvement.

If the decision to have an oversight committee is left to the government, oversight will probably be given to the Treasury Department, and the Secretary of the Treasury will probably become the leader in these matters allowing the decision-making process to be much closer to the executive branch than it is today. As we have seen, the Federal Reserve Act was brought into being to stabilize the banking system. The intent was to protect the system by protecting the banks and not the depositors. The Federal Reserve gave banks greater access to cash and would increase reserves and lower interest rates to encourage banks to make money by lending and for depositors to leave their money in the bank.

The Federal Deposit Insurance Corporation

The Federal Deposit Insurance Corporation (FDIC) was created by the Banking Act of 1933, also known as the Glass-Steagall Act. It was initially added as Section 12B of the Federal Reserve Act, making it, originally, part of the Act. In 1950, Congress separated the FDIC from the Federal Reserve. It removed Section 12B from the Act and established the FDIC as a separate, distinct independent agency.

If the Fed were abolished, we cannot rule out the possibility that as long as an adequate spread remained between the interest paid to depositors and the interest paid by borrowers, banking institutions might succeed without outside intervention, as they did for approximately 123 years, from 1790 to 1913, to a greater or lesser degree.

If they could not, it would be possible for State or national banks to enact laws which would protect primarily depositors and secondarily banks, the opposite of the Federal Reserve which protects primarily banks. One such law might be the FDIC, which would protect depositors.

If a bank experienced financial reverses, the FDIC could protect depositors rather than depending on an entity to protect the banks.

If banks become insolvent, there would be no Federal Reserve on which to fall back, and the Fed would no longer operate as Lender of Last Resort.

It is quite possible that if the Fed were abolished, the banks themselves, on a free banking basis, could undertake the currency and Lender of Last Resort functions that the Fed now performs. Banks could accept deposits, make loans, and pay interest without the necessity of a governing board.

If this were the case, each bank would have to set its own interest rates based on market rates and would not have access to reserves, outside of its branches.

A modified central banking system might be used to allow several banks to join together to set interest rates and provide reserves, which would be similar to what the Fed does now but without the ability to create money.

Enforcement Issues

When the Federal Reserve Act was considered, members of Congress and financial writers voiced their concerns. Broadly stated, they feared that the government would be giving up its control over the public's money.

In his testimony before the Senate Committee on Banking and Currency, Alfred Crozier, in his critique of the proposed legislation, made two statements. He stated that under the Act, some might engage in "the contracting of loans or increasing interest rates in concert ... [with] the banks to influence public opinion or the action of any legislative body." And that the bill "vests in the banks exclusively the dangerous power to make money among the people scarce or plenty."

Broadly stated, much of the opposition to the bill came from those who felt that bankers and businesspeople might conspire with those in the upper echelon of the Federal Reserve to use inside information gathered from the Federal Reserve to gain personal wealth or political advantage.

At its inception, the fact that the Act would lead to inflation appears to have been understood. However, the greater threat at the time appears to have been that the Act could be used by wrong doers to conspire with Federal Reserve insiders to gain personal wealth or political advantage.

Two reasons that inflation may not have been perceived, at the time, to be a great threat include the following:

Firstly, in 1913, there was less experience with inflation. For the over one hundred years before the Fed, inflation ran at approximately .4 percent per year. In other words, inflation, as a financial problem, may not have been considered to be as great a problem as it became

Secondly, the new Federal Reserve Note had some gold backing. Only currency in an amount equal to two and half times the amount of gold held in reserve could be issued. Hence, inflation, if a problem at all, may have been thought to be under control by the gold backing it initially had.

To me, it appears as if the Act was initially criticized because it was thought that it would provide a way for bankers, businesspeople, and Fed insiders to conspire together to utilize the provisions of the Act to gain personal wealth or a political advantage.

Representative Charles A. Lindbergh stated the case succinctly:

> "The financial system has been turned over to the Federal Reserve Board. That Board administers the finance system by authority of a purely profiteering group. The system is Private, conducted for the sole purpose of obtaining the greatest possible profits from the use of other people's money."

Whether the Federal Reserve Act fosters criminal conspiracies or not, one must confess that the Act does have built into it provisions which a dishonest person could use dishonestly. Knowledge of the direction of the interest rate alone could provide a dishonest person with an avenue to personal gain. As time progressed, criticism of the Act changed from one in which people were convinced that it

was an Act that fostered criminal conspiracies to one where the same people were convinced it was an Act that would lead to inflation. **After the criminal angle fell by the wayside, the Act was criticized because of its inability to prevent inflation.**

We may never learn, for certain, what, if anything, has transpired among the upper management of the Federal Reserve and the bankers and businesspeople with whom they may, or may not have had business dealings.

However, we have a significant record of the enforcement activities of the Board itself over the past many years with respect to its own employees, the employees of the Federal Reserve banks, and the numerous employees of the member banks.

If the Fed is dishonest, it has remained very busy enforcing its own rules. There are numerous examples of employees bringing home computer information, moving out of bonds and into stock when it was learned that interest rates would be lowered, and that stock purchases were made based on inside information. Some of the enforcement issues that have arisen under the Act include:

In 2017, Nicholas Berthaume, a former employee of the Board, was sentenced for installing unauthorized software on a Board server that he could remotely access from his home.

In 2024, Robert Brian Thompson, a bank examiner, pleaded guilty to committing insider trading and making false statements to his employer, the Federal Reserve Bank of Richmond. Thompson misappropriated confidential information which he used to execute trades in publicly traded financial markets.

In 2024, John Freeze, former CFO of the Bank of Jackson Hole, was banned from future work in the financial industry for receiving confidential supervisory information belonging to the Federal Reserve Board. The documents were copied at Freeze's direction from a bank owned computer to a private cloud account.

In 2020, Lawrence Rufrano, a former Federal Reserve employee, was charged with wire fraud in connection with collecting disability benefits without reporting his collection to the Federal Reserve.

In 2020, Richard Clarida, Fed Vice Chairman, rotated millions of dollars out of a bond fund and into a stock fund just prior to the Fed slashing interest rates.

In 2020, Robert Kaplan, President of the Dallas Fed, and Eric Rosengren, President of the Boston Fed, carried out several questionable financial transactions in connection with the COVID-19 pandemic. Kaplan made multiple stock trades, and Rosengren made multiple purchases and sales of REITS. Kaplan stepped down, and Rosengren retired early.

While these transactions are the types of transgressions that appear to be related to inside information possessed by the Fed, they do not show an extensive network with a vast conspiracy among the upper reaches of the Federal Reserve Board, as far as we can tell.

The Fed and the National Debt

The Federal Reserve has always taken the position that it is self-funded and does not require a Congressional appropriation. The Fed's main source of income is interest earned from the securities it acquired through its Open Market Operations. Even if the Fed makes a profit, it sends any profits it may make to the Treasury. Many writers maintain that the concept that the Fed is paid for by the taxpayers is a "myth." The Fed owns a significant portion of the national debt. The Fed obtained this "ownership," by purchasing securities in the open market and placing the funds into the reserve accounts of various banks.

It appears fairly well settled that the process engaged in by the Fed of buying securities and placing the cash into a bank's reserve account **is only a process used to manage monetary policy.** Though this process might make the Fed the "technical" owner of a portion of the national debt, it does not make it the "actual" owner. If the Fed is abolished and a committee is established to watch over the economy, such a committee will probably be a government department which will be paid for by the taxpayers.

Inflation and Deflation

The Federal Reserve Act makes it the Fed's duty to maintain the long-term growth of the monetary system commensurate with the economy's long run potential to increase production in an effort to maximize employment, stabilize prices, and have moderate long-term interest rates.

The Fed has failed with respect to price stability as it has allowed the purchasing power of the dollar to be eroded. The purchasing power of a dollar in 1790 was not much different than it was in 1913. But prices soared between 1913 and 2008 with the dollar losing much of its purchasing power. Most of the decline in the dollar's purchasing power has taken place since 1971, when we were taken off of the gold standard. Stable prices are necessary for long-term planning, borrowing, lending, tax accounting, contracts, etc.

As to inflation, the majority of the highest annual rates of inflation have occurred during the Federal Reserve period. Rates between 15 and 18 percent occurred between 1917 and 1920. Rates in the low teens occurred between 1973 and 1975 and between 1978 and 1980. The episodes of high inflation coincided with the temporary gold export embargo between

1917 and 1919 and being taken off of the gold standard in 1971. While the Fed has failed to prevent inflation, it largely succeeded in eliminating deflation, which was common during the pre-Fed years. After tightening the economy during the Great Depression, the Fed no longer used tightening but turned, instead, to inflating.

Deflation can be harmful or benign. Harmful deflation results from less spending and less demand for goods. Benign deflation occurs when the cost of production is lowered, but more goods are produced; the cost reduction is reflected in a lowering of the price of the finished product.

The Fed's record with deflation does not appear to compensate for its failure to contain inflation. It has practically extinguished benign deflation but bears some responsibility for several episodes of harmful deflation including 1930 to 1933, 1937 to 1938, and 2008 to 2009.

Beginning with Paul Volcker's second term as Fed Chairman and lasting through the term of Alan Greenspan, roughly 1984 to 2007, the decline in the volatility of the rate of inflation and the decline in the volatility of real output was thought by some to mean that the economy underwent a "Great Moderation."

It was initially thought that this moderation was due to improvements in the Fed's conduct of monetary policy. However, this was not be the case. The lessening of volatility was not the result of improvements in the Fed's policies but was instead attributed to other economic phenomena.

Contractions were somewhat more frequent before the Fed was established than after World War II and were shorter and less severe. The Fed's argument that its' operation does not cause inflation directly as it does not give out money directly but only augments bank reserves.

Prospects for the Fed

If a system could be developed that was fair, such as giving more small banks access to newly created money and broadening lending standards, there might be some middle ground. As it stands, the big banks and Wall Street receive the majority of the benefits from the Fed.

If the position were taken that the Fed is an outsized governmental apparatus which leads to class distinctions and unfairness among social and economic groups, those might be reasonable assertions, but they do not correct the banking system.

One could maintain that the population existing in the United States today could not survive without an entity similar to the Fed. The people of today have become so dependent on the government to take care of them during difficult times, ranging from natural disasters to economic difficulties that they would be unable to cope without the Fed.

People today plan for their future knowing that if things collapse, the government will protect them. This may be a sociological problem rather than a financial problem. Things were very bad during the Pandemic. But imagine what would have happened if the government had not stepped in with trillions of dollars to keep the country going?

It is said that the Fed inflates the money to combat recession. I do not believe that the Fed intentionally over-inflates but inflates as much as it deems necessary to achieve its objectives. The country, as a whole, has terrible spending habits. Millions and millions of dollars are spent on wasteful programs and wars, and the Fed needs to inflate, perhaps too much, to cover the negligent spending.

What is the bottom line?

(1) If we want a system in which an entity independent of Congress or the President keeps the economy running but does so by inflating the currency, increasing the money supply, devaluing the dollar, and generally benefiting the wealthy, we have the Federal Reserve.

(2) If we want a system which does not oversee the economy but provides only traditional banking which may allow recessions and other downturns to take place, we can eliminate the Fed and see if we do better with traditional banking in the 21st Century than we did in the 19th and 20th.

(3) If we feel that it is absolutely necessary to have an entity overseeing the economy, we could return to traditional banking for banking and create a separate governmental agency to oversee the economy and come to its aid if recession persists or threaten to ripen into a depression.

If we retain the Fed under option 1, the Fed will continue to oversee the economy and provide Open Market Operations and Quantitative Easing in times of economic stress. As to exigent circumstances, we would still have the Fed's emergency lending power set forth in Section 13(3) of the Act, bearing in mind that the extension of credit would only be available when the borrower is unable to secure credit from other banking institutions.

Under option 1, the government could still enact legislation, separate from the Federal Reserve Act, for a financial oversight committee or an emergency relief program, including an appropriation from Congress, which would be included in the national debt, with interest.

Under option 2, we would not have an entity to oversee the economy as the Fed does. Also, we would not have the Fed's emergency lending power, as it comes under the Federal Reserve Act.

Under option 2, the government could still enact legislation, separate from the Federal Reserve Act, for a financial oversight committee or an emergency relief program, including an appropriation from Congress, which would be included in the national debt, with interest. Witness: TARP.

Under option 3, we would have an oversight committee, but it would not have the same powers as the powers given to the Fed by the Federal Reserve Act to address downturns.

Under option 3, however, the government could still enact legislation, separate from the Federal Reserve Act, for a financial oversight committee or an emergency relief program, including an appropriation from Congress, which would be included in the national debt, with interest. Witness: The Cares Act.

The three options set forth above contemplate that the economy will continue to be run by banks; banks that collect deposits, pay interest, and collect interest from their borrowers, making a profit on the spread. The present system is dependent on the Fed adding money to bank reserves and encouraging the banks to loan it out at interest.

Let us consider an option 4.

Approximately 50 years before the Federal Reserve Act came into being, Abraham Lincoln, perhaps our most prophetic President, proposed the following:

"The Government should create, issue, and circulate all the currency and credits needed to satisfy the spending power of the Government and the buying power of consumers. By the adoption of these principles, the taxpayers will be saved immense sums of interest. Money will cease to be master and become the servant of humanity."

        Abraham Lincoln,
        16th President of the United States

Mr. Lincoln apparently envisioned a system in which the government, following Article I, Section 8 of the Constitution, would create, issue, and circulate all of the currency and credits needed for the government to spend and for the consumer to buy, saving the taxpayers immense sums of interest.

The government would warehouse money and loan it out. This would eliminate the middleman, i.e., the banks, and allow business to be conducted without paying the banks the immense sums of interest that they collect to loan you your own money.

Such a course would require the entire monetary system to be re-vamped, but it would provide the money needed to stimulate business while reigning in the amount of money in circulation which would reduce inflation to the .4 percent levels enjoyed prior to the Federal Reserve Act.

It is impossible to speculate whether inflation would have existed even if there had never been a Federal Reserve. I would offer that the first step would be to subject the Fed to an extensive audit. The contention that an audit might lead people to fear inflation is downright silly. If anything, it might give people insight as to how inflation occurs and how it may be remedied.

A comprehensive audit might show how the Fed could adjust its policies, or how new policies might make the financial oversight component more egalitarian. If the audit shows that the Fed could be revamped and improved, that should be done.

Some politicians favor abandoning the Federal Reserve; however, they say little about a replacement system. If abandoning the Fed and reestablishing traditional banking is felt to be realistic, it may be tried. However, the American people have become very dependent on the government during times of trouble, and I doubt whether they could live through a depression every other year.

What the Fed Does:

1. **Lender of Last Resort** – The Fed may act as the Lender of Last Resort and provide emergency loans to banks facing a liquidity crisis.
2. **Create Reserves** – The Fed may inject money into bank reserves increasing reserves and the money supply and lowering interest rates.
3. **Set Interest Rates** – The Fed may set the fed funds interest rate which influences public interest rates for mortgages, automobile loans, and credit cards.
4. **Supervise Banks** – The Fed oversees and regulates commercial banks to ensure their safety and soundness, a role that traditional banks cannot do.
5. **Monetary Policy** – The Fed controls the money supply and credit conditions to promote maximum employment and stable prices, a role that traditional banks cannot do.
6. **Act as a Bank for Banks** – The Fed's customers are other banks and the government and not the general public. It processes payments and holds deposits for banks, a role that banks cannot do.

What Traditional Banks Do:

1. **Serve the Public** – Commercial banks take deposits from individuals and businesses and provide loans directly to them.
2. **Create Money (Loans)** – When a bank makes a loan, it creates a new deposit into the borrower's account, a process distinct from the Fed's creation of reserves.
3. **Earn Profits from Lending** – Banks may make Profits by charging more for loans than they pay for deposits, whereas the Fed's primary goal is not profit making.

Conclusion

Before the Federal Reserve Act, banks engaged primarily in traditional banking, that is, accepting deposits and making loans. As the size of the economy grew, banks began to experience a liquidity crisis, that is, running out of cash for their depositors.

By 1895, the situation became so dire that J.P. Morgan had to arrange a $60 million dollar loan to keep the government from going bankrupt.

In the early 20th Century, the nation reached a crossroads: Should the economy be run by bankers or by the government? The group headed by President Woodrow Wilson, chose the government, and in 1913, the Federal Reserve was born.

Having the government run such a powerful entity has engendered various arguments for and against it and its continuation. Consider the following:

Creating Base Money (Inflation) – The Fed has the monopoly on creating base money. The Fed may create money in the form of reserves and instantly inject that money into the banking system, controlling the money supply.

Since inflation is the direct result of an increase in the money supply and since the Fed controls the money supply, it may be argued that the Fed is the sole source of inflation.

Those opposing the Fed make the argument that a fixed money supply, such as the gold standard, might better insure price stability.

Those favoring the Fed take the position that the Fed's process of quickly increasing the money supply will better combat recession than waiting for banks to make loans, a process made even slower as loans can only be made if there is a creditworthy borrower and when enough money will be left in the bank to pay its ordinary business expenses.

Setting Interest Rates – The Fed influences the fed funds interest rate by setting its target range. The Fed meets every eight months and based on financial data, determines whether it will stimulate or contract the economy. If stimulation is necessary, the Fed sets the new fed funds target range below the existing rate. The new rate will then be lower than the existing rate, which will stimulate the economy.

As the fed funds rate is generally lower than the rates available to ordinary citizens, the system is deemed unfair.

Stock Market – Another argument against the Fed is that the Fed produces a great deal of valuable inside information, such as the direction of the interest rate. This information may be used or stolen by Fed employees, which works to the benefit of some but to the detriment of the public at large.

Political – Another argument against the Fed is that because it is able to lower interest rates, a political figure might pressure it to lower rates to provide a robust economy for his re-election campaign.

Overseeing the Economy – An important function of the Fed is overseeing the economy. If recession looms, the Fed may lower the fed funds rate to stimulate the economy.

The ability to stimulate the economy helps avoid depressions. There were six depressions in the pre-Fed years and only one in the post-Fed era.

The Bottom Line - If we want an entity independent of the government to oversee the economy but which allows inflation, we have the Fed. If we want less inflation and are willing to risk periodic depressions, we can return to traditional banking.

The Muse
A Short Story

If anyone comes to the gates of poetry
and expects to become an adequate poet
by acquiring expert knowledge of the
subject without the muses' madness,
he will fail,
And his self-controlled verses will be
eclipsed by the poetry of men who
have been driven out of their minds.

Plato

Table of Contents

Chapter 1 – The Vagabond Inn: Early Summer 97
Chapter 2 – The Foster Home 102
Chapter 3 – Back at the Pool 105
Chapter 4 – Leaving Town 108
Chapter 5 – Getting to Mexico 109
Chapter 6 – Our Time in Mexico 111
Chapter 7 – The Unraveling of a Relationship 112
Chapter 8 – The Interview: Background 114
Chapter 9 – The Interview: Letters 124
Chapter 10 – The Interview: Using My Likeness 130
Chapter 11 – The Interview: Conrad's Works 143
Chapter 12 – The Interview: The Muse Factor 148

Chapter 1
The Vagabond Inn

Early Summer

The Vagabond Inn is a real dump. The pool area is so close to the highway that you never know when you might get hit by an errant hubcap while lying around the pool minding your own business.

The only, and I mean only, thing this place has going for it is a small, free-standing changing bungalow immediately adjacent to the pool area, complete with a working shower.

I took up my usual position on a well-worn chaise positioned on the far side of the pool, as far away from the highway as possible.

It was around 2 in the afternoon. It appeared as if I would be the only guest using the pool, which was not unusual.

I had a couple of magazines and the local newspaper. I organized my reading material and settled in for an hour of sun and an occasional swim. It was relatively temperate for this time of year in the Arizona desert.

I stayed in this motel because it was on the road between Tucson, where my mother was housed in an assisted living facility, and New Mexico, where I was living. I failed to mention that I chose this particular establishment because it was cheap, and I was broke.

I am a writer, and I have elected to live or die by the word. In other words, I refuse to take a side job to support my writing. Books written by first-time writers are not a great source of revenue.

As I laid back minding my own business, from the changing

bungalow the most fantastically beautiful woman emerged. I was certain that it was a hallucination. How would such a thing be possible in the middle of the nowhere?

I guess you could say that she was blondish, 5 foot, 4 inches tall, weighing 115 pounds, so not too skinny. She had the face of an angel and the body of a goddess. After her first appearance, she left the pool area. I presumed that she went either back to her room or home.

The next day, I returned to the pool area, and she again appeared. She was wearing jeans and a work shirt. She had a holster with a Colt revolver in it.

At 42, I still looked ok. My hair was still brown, and I was not fat. At that time, I would have put her age at around 19, which might have been wishful thinking on my part.

She came over to me.

I started, "So, what brings you to the middle of the desert?"

She replied, "I live in a foster home not far from here, and I come here to use the shower."

"They don't have showers at the foster home?"

"Yes, but if I shower there, the guys living or working there will try to come into the bathroom."

"You can't lock the door?"

"No. It's a foster home. There are no locks on the bathroom door."

"Sorry, I didn't know."

I continued, "By the way, what is your name?"

"I'm Alley, short for Alicia. And your name?"

"My name is Conrad."

I continued and asked, "Is that you gun?"

She was embarrassed and feared that I might try to take her gun away from her, exercising my supposed rights as an adult.

She replied, "Yes."

"Why do you have a gun? Do you intend to shoot me?"

"No. Of course not."

"Good then."

She seemed surprised that I did not reprimand her for

having a gun. The implication to me was that she was not used to having adult people reason with her but only order her around. She appeared to relax.

I asked, "So, you live in a foster home.?"

"Yes."

I asked, "Did your parents die? I have heard that often children who reach your age, when their parents die are moved to foster care, when there are no other relatives to take them in."

She replied, "No. My parents are not dead. At home everything was okay until I reached 11. At that time, my parents moved down here to Tucson from North Dakota.

"My father became an alcoholic, and he often beat me, sometimes sending me to the hospital. I was placed in foster care, but my mother, with whom I had a fairly normal relationship, stayed with him. I would go back and forth between my parents' home and foster care, moving to the foster home when my father became enraged for one reason or another and beat me. That is how I ended up in foster care. I never really blamed my father; I just figured that he could not control himself.

"Every time I was hit, I would disappear inside of myself, and it would often take weeks or months to reemerge. So, I decided that I was not going to be hit any longer. I was just going to shoot anyone who tried."

I replied, "And that would explain the gun."

She appeared to be thinking to herself that she was relieved that someone understood her situation.

She said, "I have only one friend in foster care, my roommate Ellen. Otherwise, everyone there is horrible."

In a not so veiled effort to change the subject, she asked, "Do we know each other. You look vaguely familiar. I remember now, I saw your photo on the back of a book jacket. I think the book was called *The Hidden Body.*"

"I did write that book over 10 years ago. Where did you see it?"

"Frankly, it was in a bin of used books outside of a store. I remember it was a hard cover edition. I bought if for a quarter, I think. No offense."

"No offense taken. It was my first book. I wrote two more books after that one. None of them sold very well. And that is why I am still poor and staying in a dump like this."

She said, "At the home, I hide away in my closet and read Steinbeck, Faulkner, and all of the great American novelists, of which there are not many. Your book made it into some very good company."

I replied, "That book won the Faulkner award for best novel by a new writer. I guess they don't know much about book sales and making a living."

She said, "I could never write novels."

"And why is that" I asked.

She replied, "I guess that I am too much of a realist. The great novelists are concerned with character development and interaction. The plot, when stripped down, becomes so implausible you wonder why they bothered with it at all."

"How so," I asked.

"Let's take *The Hidden Body*. In it, Martin picks up a hitchhiker named Thomas. When Thomas tries to rob him, Martin kills him. Martin dumps Thomas' body in a gravel pit on Baker's property. Rather than contacting the authorities, Baker hides the body. Thomas' wife, Maddy, and his son, John Western, vow to avenge his death.

"Martin picks up whisky from Baker's farm but drives his car into a stream. John Western, while checking some traps, comes to Martin's aid, unaware that Martin is the person who killed his father. It's quite a coincidence.

"Martin and John Western develop an almost father and son-like relationship. The local police find Martin's car in the stream. The police try to get John Western to testify that Martin was driving the car with its cargo of illegal whisky, but he refuses. The police go to Baker's house to question him.

"Baker engages in a shootout with the police and is arrested. Martin is captured and is sentenced to three years for transporting the whisky. John Western leaves town. When he returns, the town is abandoned.

"I understand at least some of the themes including the relationship between fathers and sons, guilt, civilization encroaching on rural life, and others. But in my way of thinking, in real life, when the first killing took place, Martin, who was actually acting in self-defense, would call the authorities to clear his name, and someone would arrange for the dead man to be buried.

"The owner of the farm would not hide a dead body on his property when he was not involved in the killing. He would call the coroner. Besides, a dead body, while decomposing, would create a terrible odor.

"To pursue the relationships and themes, the novelist must make at least some of the movements of his characters not plausible. If Martin and Baker had turned the dead body over to the authorities, that would have been the end of the story. It took hiding the body and crashing the car into the stream to bring John Western in contact with Martin and Baker in a way that relationships could be developed among them. Am I making any sense?"

I replied, "Yes you are making perfect sense. It's called 'literary license' and has accounted for much of the great writing in the English language, including the American novel."

"I have to get back to the home now. If I stay out any longer, I will be punished, which I hate."

I replied, "It has been such a pleasure to meet you and hear your opinions, including some not so flattering opinions about my first book. I have two more books in print now and am working on another. I'll still be here tomorrow. I stay here while I visit my mom in Tucson and then return home to New Mexico."

She replied, "I'll see you tomorrow then around the same time, if you don't mind."

I concluded, "I don't mind at all. Take care. Again, nice meeting you."

Chapter 2
The Foster Home

After she left, I caught a little more sun and then went to my room and changed my clothes. It was about 5:30 in the evening. My plan was to drive to a nearby place for dinner. But my curiosity got the better of me. I drove in the direction I saw her take on her bike to see if I could figure out which house was her foster home. By car, it did not take long. About two blocks towards town I saw what had to be the foster home.

If you thought that the motel was a dump, it does not compare to the foster home in that department. The foster home was a complete and utter disaster. It looked as if it had not been painted in 20 years. The windows were barely in place. What may have been a front lawn at one time was now dirt. The trash bins were on the east side of the house, and trash was scattered around the open bins with flies hovering nearby. How do people live like this?

I drove past as quickly as I could and reached my destination another mile or so up the road. I had dinner at a place called Pinky's. It was pretty good, and was clean inside. I had a turkey sandwich and salad.

I learned only some vague details about life in the foster home from Alley. She really had no interest in talking about it with me or with anyone else for that matter.

However, years later, after my romantic relationship with Alley had long run its course, I was contacted by Ellen Sullivan, who, according to Alley, was her only friend at the foster home. Ellen was looking for a job. By that time, I had become a successful writer and was working with the Santa Fe Institute, which often needed clerical help. I asked her to come by the Institute and speak with Ms. Spellman, the head of the clerical department. I put in a good word for her with Ms. Spellman, even though I was not certain whether she could do the job or not.

The next day, I received word from Ms. Spellman that Ellen's interview went very well and that she was given the job she was seeking. Ellen called to thank me for recommending her. I used the opportunity to invite Ellen for a drink so I could speak with her about Alley. Even though Alley and I were no longer physically involved, I remained so in love with her that any tidbit of information about her was of great interest. I listened intently as Ellen related her story about Alley and their time in foster care.

Ellen told me the following: "Our life at the foster home was horrible. Alley suffered from an affliction suffered by only a handful of women in this world, the affliction of being too attractive to men. She was not only too attractive, but she had that thing, that sexual attraction thing, that some women have, even when they don't want it, and even when they try to hide it, which was the case with Alley.

"When a man sees such a woman, he loses all control. He has to get near her. He has to possess her, even when he has no chance of obtaining her.

"In Alley's case, she could not even take a shower without men trying to break into the bathroom for the opportunity to see her awesome beauty. A woman with this power invites so much attention that she cannot live a normal life.

"Being from your background, something that you might not understand is that when you go further down on the socio-economic scale, problems in the man to woman relationship department become different. At the upper levels, men have the ability to achieve self-worth by accomplishments of their own, be they in business, sports, or entertainment. He can parlay the money he makes from such accomplishments into an aura which attracts women, even if the same man could not attract the same woman without that aura.

"If Alley had a normal life in high school and college, the young men would hopefully have enough upbringing to try to date her and then respectfully give up. Perhaps if they got drunk at a party or in a bar, they might lose their brakes and become aggressive, but they would eventually settle down.

"When men are poor, like around here, when they are rejected, they have no intellect on which to fall back. They can only deal with rejection by acting out and trying to force their way into a woman's life in an effort to appeal to her low self-esteem. When this force is rejected, it may escalate into greater force and even to physical violence, which is why there are so many cases of men beating women.

"Rejection often makes a man feel as if the woman feels that he is not good enough, which can be painful, even if it was not the woman's intent at all.

"Strange as it may sound, I even felt that her father hit her and acted the way he did out of the frustration of feeling that he was not good enough, which is really unhealthy. There were no reports of the father beating the mother.

"All of the frustration that she engendered ultimately led to men forcing themselves on her and becoming physical."

"As a woman, I can tell you that being hit by a man under these circumstances not only hurts physically but also hurts psychologically. It destroys you. The man is trying to make you feel unworthy so you will be with him. The exact opposite of what is actually happening."

Conrad asked Ellen: "How did you escape this treatment?"

Ellen replied, "Simple. I'm not beautiful. I'm nice. I have tried my best to educate myself to be prepared for a job. I have done what I can. But no one was breaking down the door to see me in the shower, like with Alley."

She continued, "As you know, she was intoxicating. As we speak, I see in your face that even after all of these years, you are still reeling from the effects of just knowing her. Imagine a man less intelligent than you trying to deal with those feelings. I question if even you can.

"I know that you still stay in touch with her and send her money and letters. It's okay. I don't think that she would have less in her life because of it."

Chapter 3
Back at the Pool

I awakened around 9. I went to Pinky's and then on to see my mother in the assisted living facility. We had a nice visit, and I left.

I had lunch and returned to the pool just before 2 o'clock, as I told Alley I would. I arranged my chaise, assembled my reading material, and waited.

When she did not show by 2:30, I presumed that she had forgotten all about me. When she arrived at 2:35, it appeared as if I was wrong.

She came over and moved the other working chaise closer to me. Perhaps I was making some headway. Again, wishful thinking.

She sat down and made the first approach. "I wanted to thank you for our nice chat yesterday. It was the first time that it seemed as if someone cared about what I thought and asked my opinion about anything."

I replied, "No. It is I who should be thanking you for listening and for having so many great ideas about my first novel."

She asked, "Have you written anything since?"

I said, "Yes. I have completed two more novels. *The Hidden Body* won an award for notable first novels. After finishing it, I received a fellowship and set sail for Europe. I received another grant which allowed me to travel around Southern Europe before landing on an island off the coast of Spain, where I wrote my second novel. After that, I wrote a third novel."

My second and third novels were very dark. The first dealt with incest and the second with necrophilia.

(I failed to mention that during my college years, I married a fellow student, my first wife, and we had a son. We divorced. I also failed to mention that while sailing around Europe, I met and married my second wife. I was still married to my second wife when Alley and I met at the motel pool, and we remained married when Alley and I traveled around Mexico. Alley did not learn that I was married until we returned from Mexico.)

Alley asked, "Are you working on anything now?"

I replied, "Yes. I have a work in progress. Its title is *Life on the River.*"

Ally asked, "What is it about?"

I replied, "It's semiautobiographical. I wrote it 20 years ago about my experiences in Knoxville on the Tennessee River, but I am re-writing it."

Ally replied, "Sounds like *Huckleberry Finn* on a different river."

I asked, "How about you. What are your interests?"

Ally replied, "I'm interested in nursing. The nurses have been so great whenever I have been brought into the hospital. Right now, my main interest is in horses. I love riding, and I love horses. They are such wonderful animals. I also enjoy shooting. Have you tried riding or shooting?"

I replied, "No. Neither. But I am fascinated by both. A writer has only what he knows to write about."

I continued, "You seem to be interested in so many things. How old are you?"

Alley replied, "Right now, I'm 16, but by the end of summer I will be 17. My birthday is September 13."

I replied, "I see. With your riding and shooting skills, not to mention your ability to understand my first novel, you seem older."

Ally replied, "Oh well. How about the book you're working on?"

I replied, "Yes." The story begins when Jim, the main character, observes the police pulling a suicide victim out of the river. Jim lives alone on a houseboat surrounded by the outer fringes of society. He left his life of luxury, rejected his parents' teachings, and abandoned the wife he met at college with whom he had a young son.

"A number of misfits come in and out of Jim's life. He becomes involved with an underage teenage girl from a poor family. She reads stories about nurses and steals away into Jim's tent for sex. She meets her demise by being crushed to death under the rocks of a landslide.

"In the end, Jim feels that his identity as an individual is affirmed by his electing to live under such poor circumstances. He decides to leave the city in search of a new life."

Alley states, "That is an interesting story. It seems to say something about lifting one's self up by his own bootstraps to find a better life."

I replied, "Yes. That is true."

Chapter 4
Leaving Town

Even though Alley was there, I could not stay in Tucson visiting my mother forever, but I did return now and then. I would leave money for Alley behind the fourth Wall Street Journal at the newspaper rack outside of Pinky's, the diner not far from the home at which we would sometimes eat.

I wrote letters to Alley. Some of these letters I sent to her and some I sent to a bar called Someplace Else for safekeeping.

This arrangement went on past her 17th birthday which, as we know was on September 13, and well into the next year. During this time, she moved back to her family home.

One night, Alley missed my call. The unspeakable had occurred. She had been hit again, and she was taken to the hospital. By the time she connected with me, I was in grief.

I remember saying to her words to the effect that if she stayed at home, they were going to kill her. I told her that I was going to Mexico, and if she wanted to come, she could. I told her that she would be safe with me. I told her that I didn't want anything from her and that if she wanted to come home at any time, I would put her on a bus.

Alley agreed.

I did add the warning that if she chose to come with me, she would have to say goodbye to this place. I told her that even if she came back a week or a month from now, it would never be the same. I told her that she needed to understand that her life would change the minute that she leaves with me.

Ally said okay and that she would come.

Chapter 5
Getting to Mexico

Taking a minor to Mexico is not a simple task. It involves a travel visa and evading the authorities. I enlisted the help of a close friend who also ran interference with Alley's mother and, possibly, the police.

Ally and I drove off in my old car to Lordsburg, New Mexico. I booked adjoining rooms. I wrote off for Ally's birth certificate which I amended on my typewriter.

Alley packed her stolen Colt revolver, her stuffed kitten, and some pot shards.

After we arrived, I asked whether she could shoot the gun she brought.

She replied, "Yeah, a little."

Alley and I went into the yard behind the motel. I arranged some bottles for target practice. When she hit all of the bottles, I was amazed, commenting on how well she could shoot. I then threw a leather strop into the air. She shot it straight through the center.

Alley thought that she had done something wrong and feared that I might send her back to Tucson. She rattled off several things which she felt would justify my keeping her. She said, "I'm very clean. I can cook. I know how to change a ribbon on a typewriter."

I replied, "Change a typewriter ribbon. That settles it, you're staying."

That afternoon we returned to the motel room and made love for the first time. I was 43, and she was 17.

I received a call from my agent who told me that the FBI had paid him a visit. They let him know that the FBI and the State of Arizona were looking for me.

I told Alley "Our relationship was discovered when your mom found some of the letters I wrote you in your room. This got them to the motel where they learned the make and license plate number of my car. Apparently, I'm wanted for statutory rape and for violating the Mann Act."

Alley said, "I am afraid that they will find me. I can't go back to that foster home. I don't want to go back to the life I had. Nobody likes to get hit. Every time someone hits me, it makes me feel like a wild animal whose leg is caught in a trap. I will chew off my leg to escape the trap and that feeling of being caught in it. I would do anything to make it stop. What will we do if they find us?"

I replied, "I will shoot them."

Alley asked, "What if there are a lot of them?"

I replied, "I will kill them."

This calmed Alley down. They would travel from El Paso to Juarez the next day.

Chapter 6
Our Time in Mexico

The time we spent together in Mexico was clearly our honeymoon phase. We disappeared into a cocoon of love of a kind that neither of us had ever known.

In May, we traveled along a path I was researching for a novel I would call Blood Money.

The path we traveled started in Juarez and moved into Chihuahua, Mexico City, Los Mochis, and Baja. As we left each town, Alley would send her mother postcards telling her that she was alright. Knowing her daughter was not in danger, she stopped cooperating with the FBI and the State police. The authorities, with no evidence, no cooperation, and no jurisdiction, discontinued their investigation. I doubt that the investigation was ever very much, though one could make a fairly strong case that laws were broken.

Mexico was idyllic and cheap. We lived like royalty, which felt odd to me as I always lived as if I was poor. Alley's blond hair captivated the Mexican children as they had never seen such hair before. She was like a teenage queen to them.

All good things must end. When Ally turned 18 on September 13, we spent her birthday in Mexico City and the next day flew back to El Paso. By that time, Alley had reached the age of consent in all 50 States.

Chapter 7
The Unraveling of a Relationship

After we returned from Mexico, we spent a few months living together in El Paso.

Unfortunately, several events took place which forever separated us romantically, though we still stayed in touch for the rest of my life, during which time my most "successful" books were written and published.

During this time and for the rest of my life, it was my custom to write letters to her. I guess that I could not help myself. I was so in love with her. When I spoke to her face-to-face, I was able to pretend that I was detached from her romantically while at the same time conveying that I was genuinely interested in her as a person and that she was always safe and secure with me. A pretty good acting job, if I do say so myself.

Unfortunately, when I wrote, I was unable to pretend. I guess it was just the writer in me. Hiding behind the written word allowed all of my emotions to flood out of my being, causing me to say too much.

I advise all of my male readers to never write to the women. It is better to leave an element of mystery. Whatever you say in a letter to a woman will not change the way she thinks about you. It will only expose you to pain and make her uneasy.

There might be a few relationships in which the woman is so completely in love with you that whatever you say, either face-to-face or in writing, will make no difference. But for the vast majority of relationships, over-expressing your feelings will only lead to unsatisfactory results.

When Alley was 18 and we returned to El Paso, she found

out that I was still married. A year later, on a trip to Las Vegas, she found out that I had a son about her age. Both of these discoveries are very bad for a relationship, particularly one such as ours in which the glue binding us together was more related to security, safety, and trust, than it was to lust.

She put me on a pedestal and finding out that I had a wife and child definitely compromised my position.

When we could no longer pay the rent in El Paso, we moved in with my good friend Will in Tennessee. Will and I were out working one day, and I was late picking up Alley. She was convinced that I was dead. When she thought that I would no longer be available to her, she feared that she could not survive on her own without me. This led her to believe that the relationship was not healthy.

Around this time, I won a very prestigious grant. This gave me have enough money to send her home to see her family. When she went home, she never came back. She didn't come back for all of the reasons outlined above, but, more importantly, I believe that she felt that she would have to learn to live by herself before she could learn to live with me.

The money I received from the grant set in motion a chain of events that forever ended our romance. I made several trips to Tucson to convince her to come back to El Paso. I even proposed marriage twice.

Though Alley and I would continue to stay in close touch for the rest of my life, we never returned to what we had.

I guess you could say that she remained in my life from the time of the re-writing of *The River* and throughout the writing of the rest of my novels and screenplays, until my passing.

Chapter 8
The Interview

Background

Throughout the relationship, and particularly after the break up, I wrote several very important novels and screenplays which were discussed in all of the colleges, universities, film clubs, book fairs, and periodicals which dealt with writing.

Reviewers, biographers, and other readers weighed in on my works, spinning their theories about why I utilized the symbolism, motivations, character development, and locations that I chose.

I had only completed three novels prior to meeting Alley. Each was a critical success, but none were financially remunerative. I only achieved financial success around the time that Alley and I parted ways romantically but agreed, at least tacitly, to stay in touch on a personal level.

I often sent manuscripts to Alley to read. From these manuscripts, she was convinced that she was the muse for my writing.

Alley declined to give interviews about me during my life. I presume that she did not want to betray my secrets and may have felt uncomfortable about admitting to a romantic relationship which was, due to my age, technically illegal, even though the Statute of Limitations had long run.

I presume that she felt that after I died, she could give an interview, which she did.

After Conrad's Death

After Conrad's death, Alley did agree to give an interview to interview to *Interview Magazine*, as she generally liked the magazine and its editorial stance on most issues.

The interview was to be held in Tucson, Arizona, where Alley was living. The date and location were arranged by Common Communications, Inc., the parent company of *Interview Magazine*. The interview would be in the office suite of one of the magazine's affiliates in Tucson.

Alley traveled to the office building, found the suite, and checked in with the receptionist. The receptionist took her into a conference room which had a large conference table in its center surrounded by large chairs on casters. A small tape recorder was placed in the center of the large table.

The receptionist, after making Alley comfortable, offered her a bottled water, which she accepted. Alley took up her position in the chair designated by the receptionist. The receptionist left the room and returned with the bottled water.

A nice looking, youngish man entered the room. He was well dressed in slacks, a sport coat, and a crisp white shirt. He took his jacket off and draped it over one of the empty chairs. He leaned over the table and turned the tape recorder on.

He addressed Alley, "Hi, my name is Jason Beck. I will be conducting the interview today, and I just want to make sure that you know that there is a tape recorder on the table and that it is turned on and recording our conversation. Is that acceptable?"

Alley said, "Yes."

Jason said, "The purpose of this interview today is to gather facts for an article which will appear in *Interview Magazine* about your relationship with the famous writer Conrad McDonald, who recently passed away. Is that your understanding?

Alley replied, "Yes. It is."

Jason said, "Good. Let's get started then."

Jason asked, "Will you please state your full name, so that

I may have it on the tape?"

Alley replied, "My full name is Alicia May Witt."

Jason asked, "Would you prefer that I address you as Alicia or Ms. Witt?"

Alley replied, "Everyone calls me Alley. I barely use Alicia. So please call me Alley."

Jason replied, "Okay. Alley it is."

Jason asked, "Do you know Conrad McDonald?"

Alley replied, "Yes."

Jason asked, "May I know for how long you knew him."

Alley replied, "From the time I was 16 until his death."

Jason asked, "Where did you meet?"

Alley replied, "We met at the swimming pool at his motel when I was 16."

Jason asked, "How did this come about?"

Alley replied, "To answer that question, I will need to provide some background about why I was at a motel pool in the first place."

Jason replied, "Please."

Alley replied, "I had a terrible childhood. My father beat me to the point where I had to be sent to a foster home. In the foster home, the men continually spied on me, particularly when I was in the shower. So, I would go to the pool at a nearby motel because it had a changing room with a shower. I would use the shower there, which gave me some privacy."

Alley continued, "One day when I emerged from the changing room I saw a man on a chaise lounge on the other side of the pool. He looked familiar, but I could not place him. I returned to the foster home. I realized that the man at the pool was the man in the photo on the back cover of a book I recently bought from a bin outside of a bookstore. The book was *The Hidden Body*, and the man was Conrad McDonald."

Jason asked, "What happened next?"

Alley replied, "I returned to the pool the next day, and he was there again. I was wearing a work shirt and jeans and had a Colt revolver strapped to my waist. He asked what the gun was for.

I explained to him how my father would hit me, and how I was treated at the foster home. I told him that I intended to never be hit again and that I intended to shoot anyone who tried."

Jason asked, "How did he reply to that?"

Alley continued, "Instead of becoming shocked and calling for someone from the motel to have me removed, he was cool about it. I will never forget what he said. After telling him that I intended to shoot anyone who tried to hit me, rather than being weird about it, he simply said, 'That would explain the gun.'

"I remember thinking to myself that I finally met someone who gets it.

"We stuck up a nice conversation, something I had not had in quite a while. We met several times, had dinner a couple of times at Pinky's, a local diner, and became, for lack of a better word, friends. He could see that I was in need, and he offered to help to the extent that he could, as it appeared as if he was not making a lot of money at that time. He told me that because he was always traveling, he would leave money and letters for me at the newsstand at Pinky's and that we could connect on the phone at arranged times. This went on well into the next year.

"Unknown to him, I was returned to my family home from foster care. During that stay, my father beat me so badly that I wound up in the hospital. Conrad and I scheduled calls because neither of us had a phone or was around a phone very much. One day, I missed Conrad's call. By the time I was able to contact him, he was upset. I told him about my hospital stay. He said that if I stayed at home, they were going to kill me. He said that he was going to Mexico, and that he wanted me to come with him. He said that if I ever wanted to come home, he would put me on a bus and send me. He also warned me that if I came with him, my life would change forever. He was very honest about it."

Jason asked, "What did you say?"

Alley replied, "I said okay, I'd come, which I did."

Jason asked, "Is this when you went with him to Mexico?"

Alley replied, "Before going to Mexico, we first went to New Mexico. Conrad ordered a copy of my birth certificate to which he made certain alterations to facilitate my getting into Mexico. While in New Mexico, Conrad asked if I could shoot. We went behind the motel where he set up some bottles as targets. I hit them all easily. He then threw a leather strop into the air, which I also hit straight through the center.

"I was afraid that my shooting might scare him away and began apologizing. It did not. That night we made love for the first time. He was 43, and I was 17. I could not imagine, after my childhood, making love for the first time with anyone but Conrad. I loved him. He was my safety. If I had not met him, I know that I would have died young. The trouble that Conrad and I had was different and came much later.

"The FBI and the Arizona State Police contacted one of Conrad's business associates about our whereabouts. They apparently connected me to Conrad through my mother who found some of the letters that Conrad had written to me in my room. They questioned people at the motel in New Mexico and obtained the license plate and make of Conrad's car. It appears as if Conrad was wanted for statutory rape and for violating the Mann Act."

Jason asked, "What was his reaction?"

Alley replied, "You mean Conrad's? He was undaunted. I was the one who was terrified, not because of what Conrad did, but because I didn't want to go back to foster care. I didn't want to go back to that way of life. I didn't want to get hit anymore. Nobody likes to get hit. Nobody.

"Conrad calmed me down by joking that if anybody tried to do anything to me, he would shoot them and kill them. He did this throughout our long relationship."

Jason asked, "What happened after the motel in New Mexico?"

Alley replied, "Conrad and I traveled around Mexico. We had a wonderful time. He worked. I played with the children and the other wonderful people we met."

Jason asked, "Why did you leave."

Alley replied, "When I reached 18, which was on September 13, the need to be in Mexico seemed to pass, and we, mostly me, decided to return to the States. We returned and moved back to El Paso."

Jason asked, "How did that go."

Alley replied, "It went just ok. When I was 18 and we were living in El Paso, I found out that Conrad was still married to his second wife. About a year later on a trip to Las Vegas, I found out that he had a son, who was about my age, with his first wife.

"Then while we were living with Conrad's friends in Tennessee, when Conrad didn't show up, I thought that something might have happened to him. He did finally materialize, but I learned something about myself. I learned that I could not survive on my own without him, and that is not love. The relationship was too unhealthy. I was also disappointed about the wife and child thing.

"After that something happened which forever changed our relationship. Conrad won a lot of money by winning a prestigious grant. This afforded him enough money to send me home. After he sent me home, I never went back.

"He made several trips to Tucson to try to convince me to come back to El Paso with him. He even proposed marriage, twice.

"But I could not return to him in that way. Even so, from the time of our parting romantically until his death, we stayed in close touch; but we were never able to re-establish the relationship we had.

"After that, as I am sure you know, he became an extremely successful writer and won numerous awards and made a great deal of money from book sales and sales of his books to be made into movies. After he got all of this money, he was never the same. But I couldn't muster up the strength to tell him how I felt until I wrote a comment to an article about one of his last books, which was way too late in our lives.

"He ultimately moved to a big spread in Santa Fe. Beginning in 2014, he was a trustee for the Santa Fe Institute, a scientific research center."

Jason, slightly changing his tone, said, "You do understand that this is a magazine interview and that magazine publishers are in the business of selling magazines. As magazine sales grow, so does advertising revenue."

Alley replied, "I understand."

Jason said, "This means that I will have to ask you some tough questions as there are things about your relationship with Conrad which my bosses feel might be of interest to some of our readers."

Alley replied, "I understand."

Jason said, "Let me begin with this. Throughout Conrad's long career, there have been several articles written about him. These articles have generated comments from various corners of the reading world.

"Many comments from readers seem to center around the age difference between you and Conrad. He was 42, and you were 16 when you met. Some people have taken the view that he groomed you to become his lover. They maintain that you were too young to make an informed decision on your own and that you could be easily manipulated by someone as worldly and sophisticated as he. I understand that people have their own preconceived notions about such things as age differences in a relationship, but in your opinion do any of these misgivings apply in the case of you and Conrad?"

Alley replied, "No. In fact, nothing could be further from the truth. I cannot speak for every 17-year-old girl. I was 17, almost 18, when Conrad and I first consummated our relationship. There may be some who could be persuaded that his conduct might be considered grooming, but I am not one of them, at least in our relationship. He saved me. I loved him, and he loved me. Making love was, therefore, natural and felt right."

Jason replied, "But you were under 18, and the only defenses to statutory rape would be either that the participants were close in age, which you were not, or that the perpetrator did not know your correct age, which he did."

Alley replied, "I was 17, but I turned 18 just a couple of months after our first encounter. It is also interesting to note that our first encounter was in New Mexico where the age of consent is 16, under most circumstances.

"I find it fascinating that if a man has sex with a 17-year-old in some States, he is called a pedophile. However, if they travel a few miles or even a few blocks into another state, the same man may have sex with the same 17-year-old, and it will be perfectly legal, depending on the age of consent in the second State. You might be interested to know that the age of consent is 18 in only 13 States. It is under 18 in 37 States.

"But the 7-year Statute of Limitations has long past for Conrad, and he is now deceased. The only reason that I granted this interview at all is because Conrad has passed, and he does not have to hear about his reputation being soiled by people who prefer to put him down rather than understand that he saved my life, which was the important thing to me.

"If he had not become such a famous and successful writer, the people who write comments would not pay attention to him at all. Remember, at the time of our first encounter, he was broke. I loved him for loving me and saving me, and not for his money or success, as others have done in his later years. In fact, his financial success did more to drive a wedge between us than it did to bring us together.

"I can't imagine, after the childhood I had, making love for the first time with anyone but Conrad. It all felt right. It felt good. I loved him. He was my safety."

Jason said, "It seems as if I have hit a nerve with the questions about your age difference."

Alley replied, "Really? You give yourself too much credit. You did not hit a nerve. Hitting a nerve implies that you have done something clever. You have not. You have only shown that, similar to many popular magazine writers, you have a need to lapse over to the salacious rather than to present the subject.

"In your defense, I cannot say that a 17-year-old having sex with a 40-year-old is always a good thing. I do, however, believe that the court of public opinion might be well served to look at the totality of the circumstances rather than just the chronological age difference. It is possible for two people of different ages to have a legitimate relationship worth allowing. This is particularly the case in the United States where the age of consent is so vastly different in the several States.

"I cannot say that I didn't have my personal problems with Conrad, but those problems were not because we were lovers when I was just under 18.

"No, my problems with Conrad stemmed from letters he wrote me throughout our relationship, including during times when we were not romantically involved and how he used a fictionalized version of me in his books. Those are legitimate problems. Our physical relationship is really not, except to the extent that it was a positive thing for me, and, I presume, for him as well.

"I do hope you realize that I am defending the one man who ever defended me. I think you can understand that."

Jason replied, "I understand."

Alley said, "So, allow me to turn the tables here and ask you a tough question. Aside from the statutory rape references, did you see anything in the comments which you thought might be of actual, legitimate interest?"

Jason replied, "Yes, I did. I saw a photograph of you and Conrad somewhere in the snow when you appear to be about 17, and he appears to be a youngish-looking 40-year-old. It looks as if you were staying in this place, but I am not sure.

"In this photo, you are standing very close to him, and he has his arm around you. Your head, with its blonde hair, is pressed back against his upper chest just below his shoulder. You are both smiling. My point is that you both look happy and content with one another; there was no implication that you were being forced in any way, either physically or mentally.

"What I mean to say is that hearing that a 40-year-old man is with a 17-year-old girl might sound strange. But when I saw the photograph of the two of you, it just looked normal."

Alley replied, "We had a wonderful time at that place. He made me feel so safe."

Chapter 9
The Interview

Letters

Jason continued, "Now that we have the age thing out of the way, let's hear about the letters and the use of your likeness in his books.

"You say that Conrad wrote you many letters throughout your long relationship, I mean during your relationship both when it was romantic and when it was not, such as the period between your breakup and Conrad's death."

Alley replied, "Yes, throughout the course of his life, after meeting me and until he died, he wrote letters to me, some of which were sent to me and some of which were sent to a business associate for, I think, safekeeping."

Jason asked, "Was there anything odd about the letters?"

Alley replied, "The first thing I noticed was how differently he spoke to me face-to-face compared to how he spoke to me in his letters."

Jason asked, "What did he say about that?"

Alley replied, "He said that he was a writer and that as a writer, he was used to expressing his feelings in writing and that this was why his written communications were so vastly different from his face-to-face communications."

Jason said, "You were so kind as to allow me to read many of the letters. May I ask you about them or should we change the subject?"

Alley replied, "No. I understand that the letters will be important to the public in evaluating Conrad so I will do my best to answer your questions. The letters are going to be made public in a few months, so it is better that I supply background rather than allowing someone else to try."

Jason said, "I agree with that."

Before the interview could continue, Alley insisted on a round of target practice. She insisted that I get up to speed with the use of a non-lethal firearm legal in every State without a permit. We drove to a small park adjacent to the bike trail. Alley picked out a sign across the trail we could use as a target.

She took a few shots. I commented on what a good shot she was. I asked if she and Conrad ever went shooting. She said that he did not like to shoot but that he loved to watch her shoot and to buy her guns. She had several.

After several shots, we returned to the office and took up our seats in the conference room.

I returned to the subject of the letters. I said, "The letters appear to have started when you were around 17 and continued for 47 years until Conrad's death, quite a long time."

She replied, "Yes."

I said, "In his letters, he writes about you so erotically, but I understand that many of the letters were written when your relationship was not yet romantic or after your relationship was no longer romantic. All of the letters, whether written during the period when you were romantically involved or during the periods when you were no longer romantically involved, ended with 'I love you.' What did you make of this?"

Alley replied, "I would have to say that I found that the erotic letters, particularly those written during the times when we were not romantically involved, were difficult."

Jason asked, "Did you ever talk to him about the letters?"

Alley replied, "Yes."

Jason asked, "What did he say?"

Alley replied, "As I said before, he said that as a writer, he was used expressing his more complex feelings in writing. He said that he found it impossible to communicate such feelings face-to-face."

Jason asked, "May we look at a couple of examples of the

letters?"

Alley replied, "It has been years since I've looked at them. I cannot remember exactly what was said. But hearing some passages from the letters might help your readers understand the relationship, which is important to understanding him."

Jason said, "Well, allow me to give it a try. Conrad says in one letter, 'You'd be enormously sexy speaking French. Of course, you are enormously sexy speaking English. Or making hand signs. Or just rolling your eyes. Or stone mute. Or asleep. I keep wanting to tell people about you. Stop strangers in the street. I'm a little gone on the subject.'"

"In another letter he says, 'Been thinking about you steadily all day today. Very bad withdrawal symptoms. You are becoming something of an abstraction and I don't think that's so good. Need flesh and blood. Touch and feel. I have trouble coming to grips with the reality of you. I need to see you very badly.'"

"Speaking of a dream he writes, 'Very bad pangs of missing you this evening. I had sexy dreams about you all night. I sneaked you into my room. I knelt before you like a knight at an alter and pressed my face between your thighs.'"

"In another letter he says, 'Lady Blue Eyes do you miss me at all. Do you know that I am pretty well hooked on that incredibly feminine aura you exude? You are the supreme ambassador of your sex.'"

"In another letter, when speaking about you being beaten, which was before you and he became intimate, he says, 'For the absolute life of me I cannot understand how anybody could raise their hand to you. I think there is something about your beauty and your innocence that outrages a certain type of mentality. Their experience of the world is bitter and cynical and they won't have it confounded and refuted by your existence. Your simple presence is some kind of intolerable contradiction.'"

Jason paused and said, "Are you interested in my take on the letters?"

Alley replied, "Yes. Of course."

Jason said, "My take is that he feels unworthy of you. It seems to me as if he is insecure about even the potential of a relationship with you. It seems to me that he feels as if you are way too good for him, even out of his league."

Alley asked, "Really?"

Jason replied, "Believe it or not, it is not unusual for a man to feel that he is not good enough to be with a particular woman. This is the feeling that drives men to purchase diamond rings, cars, elaborate houses, and dinners at fancy restaurants. The man is using what he has, usually money, to improve his chances of being with a woman. It's as old as time."

Alley replied, "I didn't know that, but I see your point. He constantly left me money with his letters. He bought the Cadillac I am driving."

Jason continued, "These feelings of inadequacies are even more prevalent when there is a significant age difference. Older men feel that they need to give things to achieve a relationship, even friendship. They grossly overcompensate."

Alley said, "That is most interesting, and it makes sense."

Jason asks, "How about the letters?"

Alley replied, "The letters are certainly as bold, erotic, and revealing as I remember, particularly those written when we were not romantically involved. My feeling about his letters could be applied to my feelings about any letters written between two people who were romantically involved."

Jason asks, "And how's that?"

Alley replied, "Men and women have completely different reasons for entering into relationships. Even if a woman is not head-over-heals attracted to a man, she might enter into a relationship with him because she is interested in what he has to say or she needs his protection or his support, or she needs him to save her from an enemy. Romance might not be her primary interest.

"Men, on the other hand, typically enter into relationships

primarily for romantic reasons. Men are much more visual than women. Men take it on faith that the other facets of the relationship, such as being interested in what the woman has to say, will materialize, even if they don't.

"Once a man is hooked, he is done; he will hang on to his romantic feelings until the end. A woman, on the other hand, can drop the whole thing if the initial reason for entering into the relationship fades.

"My advice to a man would be to not reveal your deep, romantic feelings to a woman, unless you and she are around the same age and it is absolutely obvious that she feels the same way. If there is any chance, and I mean any chance, that she does not feel the same way, you will be much better off not communicating your feelings, even if it is hard to do.

"It would be better for you to maintain an air of aloofness, an air of pretending to not care. If instead of being overly expressive you offer an air of mystery, she may never love you, but she might respect you. If you pour your unrequited feelings out into the open, she will never do either, and there is nothing worse than losing someone's respect.

"In my case with Conrad, we were very apart in age. I certainly appreciated him and everything that he did for me. But now that I look back at the letters and how uncomfortable they make or made me feel, I begin to question my feelings, and that makes me sad."

Jason said, "You said that after you turned 18, the two of you left Mexico and returned to El Paso. Conrad received a great deal of money for winning a grant. Now that he had money, at your request, he sent you home. He made several trips to your home in Tucson to try to convince you to come back to El Paso, but you declined. Even so, you and he stayed in close touch until the end of his life.

"I have to say that at least one of the letters that I have seen from this period would be the type of letter that one might send when he was greatly hurt. In this letter he says, 'I have to confess that in a way I was hoping that I wouldn't hear from you anymore.' He went on, 'I have to confess too that there are times when I feel enormous resentment toward you ... there was nothing wrong with our love. You just threw it away ... everything is just empty.'"

Alley asked if she could read some of Conrad's letters that I had. After reading through a few, she said, "I hate to say it, but ... I think Conrad really did love me." She then said, "I had no family stability, I was homeless, I was vulnerable, I was young." She then said jokingly, "Who could blame him?" She then added, facetiously, "What a groomer!"

Chapter 10
The Interview

Using My Likeness

Jason said, "After you split with Conrad, the history I have is that you attended the University of Arizona, spent some time in a psych ward, worked at bars, became a nurse, trained horses, had a short marriage, and suffered depression and low self-esteem.

"For the rest of his life, Conrad visited you several times in Tucson and stayed at the Vagabond Inn, where you met.

"It has been reported that one time when you were depressed, Conrad came and taught you stone-masonry. Later that year, he sent you a draft for a play called the *Stoneman*.

"After that, Conrad married his third wife. They had a son, his second child.

"Many have maintained that you were Conrad's muse as well as his inspiration and the love of his life.

"As his muse, his inspiration, and the love of his life, does it not seem a little improbable that he would marry someone else and have another child?"

Alley replied, "I cannot argue with you there. But you might bear in mind that my supposed role as his muse and the love of his life were designations assigned to me by other people and were not designations assumed by me and then announced to the world. Writers, reviewers, and modern-day philosophers came up with the idea that I was his muse.

"I suffered from depression and low self-esteem. It's difficult to take the position that I considered myself to be the muse of a famous writer. If others felt it necessary to assign that designation to me, there is nothing I can do about it."

Jason replied, "A point well taken. Perhaps we should examine various of his books together to see how you fit into his writing before you become known as his muse."

Alley said, "Fair enough. But be advised that when Conrad and I spoke about specific books, which we did on several occasions, while I am sure that he felt that the conversations and visits were made out of love, sometimes I felt that he was not operating out of love but that he was doing research for his next book, including a new fictional version of me."

Jason said, "As a writer myself, I could offer excuses for him. As a writer, the only material I have on which to base my characters are the people I know. Such people provide the avenue I have to study how characters interact, and the interaction of the characters is the most important feature of fiction. Otherwise, books of fiction would be dependent on plot, and as we all know, great fiction writing has always been about characters and has not been about the plot. Some of the plot elements are downright silly, as we shall see as we examine Conrad's works."

Alley said, "That's an interesting point. Perhaps I am being a little too hard on Conrad. I have been so scrupulous about my actual relationship with him and our 26-year age difference and so determined to keep our relationship from being misunderstood by the public at large that I have forgotten that he has a limited number of actual relationships on which to base his fiction, and ours may have been one of them."

Jason replied, "That's a good starting point towards understanding your relationship with him and also with understanding the fictional relationships among his characters, which might be based, at least partly, on you.

"Let's move through the novels. Hopefully, they might shed some light on you, on him, and on his motivations.

"The first three novels, *The Hidden Body* and the second and third novels, were completed prior to you and Conrad meeting.

The fourth novel, *The River,* was started prior to your meeting but was re-written, in part, after you met, if I am not mistaken."

Alley replied, "That's correct. And it should be noted that Conrad added some characters to *The River* after we met."

Jason said, "As I recall *The River* was about Sam, the main character, and his life on the local navigable river. Sam leaves his life of luxury, rejects his parents' teachings, and abandons the wife he met at university with whom he had a son.

"The character added after you and he met he named Amanda. She is an underage teenage girl who reads stories about nurses and secrets herself into Sam's tent in the early morning hours for sex. She is killed when crushed to death by a landslide.

"Would you say that the Amanda character was added because of you?"

Alley replied, "I would have to say yes. He knew that I had an interest in nursing. Amanda was underage, as I was when he and I met. Also, he attempted to make himself look good by maintaining that she would be so enamored with him that she would sneak into his tent for sex."

Alley continues, "Often, and disturbingly, Conrad stresses Amanda's youth with references to her child's breath and her holding her arms aloft like a child for him to raise her nightshirt over her head to undress her.

"From what I can see from the book, the relationship both horrifies and excites Sam. He says that the first time that they had sex he felt giddy, but he also felt a little sorrow when he pulled down her drawers.

"Despite his guilt and attempts to break off the relationship, which Amanda refused to do, he manages to achieve happiness.

"The death part for me is really creepy. Throughout his books, the female characters die in odd and sometimes violent ways. This always made me feel uneasy, starting with Amanda in *The River.*"

Jason said, "Perhaps death was the only a logical conclusion under the circumstances."

Alley replied, "Perhaps it was, but it is still creepy to me because it relates to me."

Jason asked, "Do you know that you have been described sometimes as a 'badass Swedish-American cowgirl?'"

Alley replied, "I have heard that."

Jason asked, "I presume that you also know that though Conrad is considered one of the great writers of westerns, he would not have known anything about either horse-back riding or shooting without the knowledge he gained from you. It has been said that you taught him everything he knows about shooting and horses. Is that true?"

Alley replied, "Yes, that is quite true. He never rode or shot before or after meeting me, but after meeting me, he enjoyed watching me do both."

Jason said, "I find it quite interesting that Conrad became one of the most celebrated writers in the western genre without much first-hand experience with the west, with guns, or with horses. It reminds me of observations made by Somerset Maugham in an essay contained in a collection of essays called *The Vagrant Mood.*

"One of the essays is entitled 'The Decline and Fall of the Detective Story.' In it, Maugham takes the position that great detective stories were written by authors who were themselves actual detectives in real life. In this category he lists Raymond Chandler and Dashiell Hammet.

"He opines that being a real-life detective gives their novels an element of reality which cannot be achieved by writers who were not themselves detectives. Mr. Maugham was a British intelligence agent during the First War from where he derives his credibility for such works as *Ashenden: Or the British Agent.*

"But Conrad became a successful writer of westerns, of drug dealing, and of crime without much real-life experience in any of them.

"But enough about that. Let's get back to the interview. Did you ever feel manipulated by Conrad's obsession to tell and retell your life story in fictional form?"

Alley replied, "Yes. Often. It seems that the relationship between a writer and his muse can be quite parasitic."

Jason asked, "Was Conrad a drinker?"

Alley replied, "Not for most of his life. But he did return to drinking later in life."

"Did he take drugs?"

"No. But we tried Peyote in Mexico but stopped using it shortly after trying it."

Jason asked, "Did you know that just before you met Conrad and left for Mexico, he was still married to his second wife, though the marriage was in trouble. Did you know also that he had been traveling around the U.S.-Mexico border looking for material for one of his next novels?"

Alley replied, "No. At the time we left for Mexico, I did not know either. I did not learn that he was married until after we returned from Mexico and were living in El Paso. And I did not learn that he had a son around my age until after that.

"Around this time, he won a very prestigious grant. With the money from the grant, he was able to send me home. I went home, but I didn't return. We split up at that time because I felt that I could no longer trust him, and trust was the primary thing we had between us. We did, however, stay in touch for the rest of his life. However, during the time between our breakup and his death, when we did communicate, I always felt as if he was doing research."

Jason continued, "Conrad then wrote *Wild Horses*. This book catapulted him from an unknown writer who managed to achieve some critical acclaim to a well-known writer who achieved financial success as well as critical acclaim, with some of his novels being made into films.

"*Wild Horses* tells the story of Jack, a 16-year-old, who grew up on his grandfather's ranch in Texas. When his grandfather dies, Jack and his friend Daniel decide to travel to Mexico to work as cowboys.

"Just before entering Mexico, they meet Billy. When Billy's horse runs off during a storm, the three travel to a nearby town to retrieve the horse. The three are pursued by the authorities. Jack and Daniel escape, but they are separated from Billy.

"While still in Mexico, Jack and Daniel find work as ranch hands. Jack is promoted to horse trainer. Jack begins an affair with Alexandria, the ranch owner's beautiful daughter. Alexandria's aunt suspects that Jack and Alexandria are having an affair and cautions Jack about the consequences of a woman losing her honor in Mexican society.

"The authorities come to the ranch and arrest Jack and Daniel. They learn that after they separated from Billy, he recovered the horse but when he returned to the town to retrieve his pistol, he shot and killed a man. Jack and Daniel are taken to the same holding cell where Billy was taken. The three boys are interrogated and beaten. While they are being transferred to a larger prison, Billy is taken away and executed.

"When Jack recovers, he is freed. He also learns that Daniel survived and was freed. They discover that Alexandria's aunt interceded to free him but only on condition that Alexandria never see Jack again.

"Notwithstanding the aunt's admonition, Jack sees Alexandria anyway. She declines his marriage proposal because she must keep her promise to her family.

"Jack, on his way back to Texas, kidnaps the captain and forces him to return the horses and guns that were taken from Jack. Rather than killing the captain, Jack turns him over to a group of Mexicans. Jack finds Billy's horse. He gains legal ownership of the horse in a court hearing in which he is absolved of his other crimes."

Jason asks, "I presume that you have read this book?"

Alley answers, "Yes. Conrad sent me the manuscript. The first thing I noticed, of course, was the title. From the title, I knew what the book would be about.

"As I started reading it, I could see that the book is so full of me, but it's not me. I was so confused. Reading about Billy being executed was very sad.

"I remember thinking to myself that I was such a lover of books that I was surprised that it didn't feel good at all to read a book that was about me. Instead, I felt violated. All of my painful experiences were rearranged into fiction.

"I didn't know how to talk to Conrad about it because he was the most important person in my life. I wondered if all I was to him was a train-wreck to write about. I was trying to fix what was broken about me, but his writing was the opposite of fixing.

"Conrad called me and asked me what I thought about the book. I replied that it was beautiful, but because it included my stuffed kitten, my Colt, and everything else, it felt weird.

"Also, Billy's death made me cry for days. When he heard that, he said he knew that it would. I asked him whether he could have written the book and allowed Billy to live. He replied, succinctly, 'No, I couldn't.'"

"Alley continued, "Remembering back to times long past, I asked Conrad: 'You'll still kill people for me though, right?' He said that he would, and that was enough for me."

Jason continued, "Conrad's next novel was the *Cities of the Desert*. In it, Jack, the main character from *Wild Horses* and Jake, a character from another of Conrad's books, work together on a cattle ranch in New Mexico, not far from El Paso.

"During a visit to a brothel in Juarez, Jack falls in love with a young, epileptic prostitute, Margarita. The couple plan to marry and live in the United States. However, the brothel is owned by Jorge, who also loves Margarita.

"On the day that Margarita and Jack plan to cross the Rio Grande, Jorge has his subordinate murder the girl by cutting her throat. After Jack finds her body in the morgue, he faces Jorge in a knife fight. Though Jack kills Jorge, he is also mortally wounded."

Jason continued, "In real-life, around this time, Conrad married his third wife. She was 32 years younger than he. As I recall, you are 26 years younger. It has been reported that during their marriage, his fiction became softer.

"It has also been said that when the third marriage began to fail, which it did, his writing turned back to the very dark. This new dark phase was on display in his next book, *No Place for the Elderly.*"

Jason continued, "In this book, while hunting in the desert, the main character, Tom, comes across a drug deal gone bad. He finds a brief case filled with 2 million dollars in cash. He takes the brief case home. He tells his wife Betty Jane to go and stay with her mother, which she does.

"Anthony is hired to retrieve the money. Tom moves to a motel. Using the tracking device in the brief case, Anthony tracks Tom to the motel. Anthony kills three people, but Tom escapes with the brief case. Anthony tracks Tom to another motel in Eagle Nest. A gun fight ensues, and Tom and Anthony are both injured.

"A bounty hunter, Karl, visits the wounded Tom in the hospital and offers to give him protection in exchange for the money. Tom declines.

"Anthony ambushes the bounty hunter. As the bounty hunter pleads for his life, Anthony shoots him and then takes a phone call from Tom. Anthony vows to Tom that he will kill Betty Jane unless Tom gives him the money.

"Tom plans to meet Betty Jane to give her the money and to hide her from danger. Betty Jane's mother unwittingly reveals Tom's location to a group of Mexicans. The Mexicans kill Tom. The sheriff and Betty Jane arrive at the location at which they were to meet Tom, only to find him dead.

"Betty Jane returns from her mother's funeral to find Anthony waiting for her. Anthony says that he must fulfill his vow to kill her but offers a coin toss. Betty Jane refuses saying that he will be responsible for her fate. It is uncertain whether Anthony kills Betty Jane or not. However, when he killed the bounty hunter, he was very mindful of blood running over the ground to his boots. In the scene with Betty Jane, he checks his boots for blood which implies that he also killed her.

"Before killing her, Anthony makes a telling statement to

Betty Jane. He says, 'Your husband had the opportunity to save you. Instead, he used you to try to save himself.'

"When Tom and Betty Jane were married, she was 16, and he was 33. She had a difficult relationship with her family and looked to Tom as her savior. They meet at the Walmart where she was working."

Alley said, "But the age difference and difficulty with her family remind me of me. It is not a very uplifting story."

Jason replied, "That is true, but it was made into a very successful film."

Jason continued, "The next writing was a screenplay called *The Attorney*. In it, a Texas attorney is planning his participation in his first drug deal.

"The Attorney attends a party thrown by the drug dealer, Rainer, and his girlfriend, Mary. At dinner, the Attorney proposes marriage to his girlfriend Lana, and she accepts.

"The Attorney meets with Wes, an associate of Rainer's, to deliver the drug money. Mary sees an opportunity to steal the drugs. She contacts the Lineman for this job. The drugs are in a truck. A biker has the component necessary to start the truck. The Lineman comes up with a plan to steal the component by stretching a line across the road and decapitating the biker. The Lineman is successful. He obtains the component and steals the truck.

"After the drugs are stolen, Wes meets with the Attorney to notify him of the biker's death and the theft. Wes explains to the Attorney that with the biker dead and the cocaine stolen, the cartel will blame him. Wes suggests that the Attorney leave town. The Attorney calls Lana and arranges to meet her in another State.

"While transporting the drugs, the Lineman is pulled over by two cartel members posing as police officers. A gunfight ensues resulting in the death of the Lineman and one of the two cartel members. The surviving cartel member drives the truck to its final destination. The cartel kidnaps Lana.

"The Attorney contacts a high-ranking cartel member to

plead for Lana's life. The cartel member advises the Attorney that he needs to resign himself to the fate that he created by his choices. Even though the Attorney is willing to exchange his own life for Lana's, it was too late for her.

"The Attorney remained in Mexico. He receives an envelope under the door which contains a disc. He presumes that the disc is a snuff film of Lana. In another location, Lana's headless body is dumped into a landfill.

"Mary tracks Wes to London. She hires a woman to seduce him and steal his bank codes. She then hires someone else to steal Wes's laptop and kill him. Mary meets her banker in a restaurant and explains how she wishes to have the accounts handled. She plans to move to Hong Kong."

Alley said, "Not much of an ending for Lana."

Jason replied, "True."

Alley said, "One part troubled me."

Jason asked, "What was that?"

Alley replied, "You know that Conrad proposed to me twice. And you know that he backed out both times. In the movie *The Attorney*, which we know was adapted from a screenplay written by Conrad, when the Attorney proposes to Lana, the language he uses is virtually the same language as the real-life language he used in his proposal to me. It went like this:

   The Attorney : I intend to love you until I die.
   Lana   : Me first.

"Let me ask you, if you proposed to your girlfriend, wouldn't you find it weird if you saw the exact same words you used in your real-life proposal also used in a work of fiction?"

"To me, it was really depressing and annoying."

Jason replied, "I see your point. I have to agree that I would not like it if someone used my heartfelt proposal as fodder for his fiction."

Jason continued, "If I am not mistaken, Conrad had a relatively long period during which he did not publish very much."

Alley replied, "Yes. That is correct."

Jason continued, "His last two books, *The Diver* and *Sarah Geller,* are companion works. They were started early on in his career but were not published until just before his death.

"However, before we get into those books, we should probably discuss Conrad's growing interest in science."

Alley replied, "Yes. Sometime around 20 years prior to his death, Conrad became interested in science. In an interview with a famous talk show interviewer, he told her that he did not socialize with many writers as he preferred to converse with scientists."

Jason asked, "That is what I heard. I also heard that he became a trustee for the Santa Fe Institute, a scientific research center. Is that true?"

Alley replied, "Yes, and unlike most members, Conrad did not have a scientific background."

Jason asked, "Did he ever try nonfiction?"

Allie replied, "Yes. He wrote a book about the unconscious mind."

Jason said, "According to my understanding, *The Diver* was announced at a multimedia event hosted by the Santa Fe Institute, and that the book was influenced by the time he spent with the scientists. The New York Times reported just two years prior to his death that *The Diver* would be released and that the second novel would be released just a few months after that."

Jason asked, "Did you have an opinion about the Institute?"

Alley replied, "I thought that the Institute was unfair with Conrad. I guess that even though we were not together, I was always protective of him, for no apparent reason. When Conrad gained personal financial success, our relationship seemed to change. Maybe I was so insecure that I did not think he needed me. Also, it was easier to just step away than to confront the problem. He married his third wife, and they had a son. There was no need for me to be around."

Jason continued, "Well, perhaps we can carry on with *The Diver* and *Sarah Gellar.* The two books center around a brother and a sister, Robby Eastern and Alice Eastern.

"Both siblings were math prodigies. They grew up in east Tennessee where their father worked on the Manhattan Project with J. Robert Oppenheimer. Alice studied at the University of Chicago. Robby dropped out of Cal Tech to pursue race car driving. An accident put him out of the car racing business. The book contains italicized chapters about Alice's treatment for schizophrenia.

"In *The Diver,* Robby becomes a salvage diver operating in the Gulf of Mexico and the American South. He is haunted by his father's contribution to the development of the atomic bomb and by his inability to save his sister from committing suicide a decade earlier, for, apparently, the same reason.

"Robby conducted a salvage dive to recover any survivors of a submerged airplane that crashed. He discovered that the pilot's flight bag and data box were missing. Within a few days, two agents visit him at his apartment to question him about the missing items. He learned that there was a tenth passenger who remained missing.

"Bobby spent time in bars in New Orleans with old friends discussing philosophy and science. He visited his grandmother's home in Tennessee.

"Her house was searched two years before, and his father's research papers and family records were taken. Bobby went into hiding from the authorities.

"At the end of the novel, Bobby lies in bed writing a letter to his sister, the love of his life. He believes that he will see her again when he dies.

"*Sarah Gellar* was the companion novel to *The Diver.* It was the final novel published before Conrad's death. The novel follows Alice Eastern, the other math prodigy, who, similar to her brother, is conflicted about her father's contribution to the atomic bomb. The novel is set in Black River Falls, Wisconsin, at Stella Maris, a hospice facility for psychiatric patients.

"The novel consists of a series of conversations between Alice and her psychiatrist. The book is set up similar to a play but with no staging. The subjects included mathematics, quantum mechanics, music theory, and philosophy."

Chapter 11
The Interview

Conrad's Works

Jason continues, "From our discussion, it appears as if you believe that Conrad used you as an inspiration for some of his characters in his works of fiction, his muse, if you will, and I know that this would, at times, bother you. You have even gone so far as to imply that this practice led to your depression and a lack of self-esteem.

"Perhaps we should take another look at some of his works to assess how they more directly relate to you. Would that be satisfactory?"

Alley replied, "I have been under the impression that the point of our discussion has been to explore my 'muse status' and to bring out aspects of my relationship with Conrad after he passed in hopes that the general public will finally understand that he was never anything but kind to me. He never groomed me for sex. When sex came, it was perfectly consensual. But I understand that people could have the impression that he was some kind of pedophile who took advantage of me. I want people to know that this was not the case."

Alley continued, "To that end, allow me to turn the tables on you and ask you a question. My question to you is this: Will exploring how Conrad used me in his fiction contribute to a better understanding him, of me, of his work, and of the way he is perceived by others."

Jason replied, "I think it will."

Alley replied, "Fair enough."

Jason said, "Okay then, let's start with the books and your part in them."

Alley replied, "Okay."

Jason continued, "I thought that we would look at *The Hidden Body, The River, Wild Horses, Cities of the Desert, No Place for the Elderly, The Attorney, The Diver,* and *Sarah Geller.*

"*The Hidden Body* and the next two novels were written before you and Conrad met. It is my understanding that *The River* was written prior to your meeting but was at least partially re-written after you met.

"In *The River* the protagonist rejects his parents' teachings and abandons his wife and infant son, which is similar to what Conrad did in real life. Also, in real life, after leaving his first wife and child, he married a second wife with whom he had no children. Conrad remained married to the second wife while you and he were traveling in Mexico and after you and he returned to the States where you were still living together. You did not learn of the child with his first wife for another year or so after your return from Mexico.

"I understand that after meeting you, he introduced the character of Amanda into the book. She was an underage teenage girl, not unlike yourself. She reads stories about nursing, and we know that nursing was one of your interests. The girl enters the main character's tent in the early morning hours for the purpose of having sex. She dies when she is crushed to death under the rocks of a landslide.

"Introducing the underage girl into the story with the sexual element appears to reflect your real-life relationship with Conrad. If you and Conrad were having sex, it may have been an ego thing to include the sexual relationship in the book. If you were not, perhaps Conrad was engaging in some wishful thinking.

"Amanda's violent death is a little more complicated. If he had strong feelings for you, which, by all accounts appears to have been the case, one would think that in the book, he would allow his young girlfriend to live. But that would not be the case. There would, instead, be a violent death. But from where does the need for a violent death come? Did Conrad have deep-seated insecurities when it came to you? Or was he feeling guilty simply for being with an underage girl?"

Alley replied, "Those are interesting questions. I sometimes felt that he may have had some inner hostility towards me. I think that may have contributed to my depression. What better way to vent hostility towards a character than to kill her for no reason?"

Jason continued, "Conrad's next two works concerned the exploits of his characters along the Mexican border. Two of these works were *Wild Horses* and *Cities of the Desert*.

As we recall, *Wild Horses* tells the story of Jack and his best friend Daniel traveling to Mexico to work as cowboys. They meet Billy who has a significant horse and a vintage Colt pistol who accompanies them to Mexico. During a storm, the horse becomes missing. Billy enlists Jack and Daniel to help him retrieve the horse. In the process, Billy kills a man. Billy is apprehended, but Jack and Daniel escape and find employment on a ranch.

"While working with the horses at the ranch, Jack encounters the owner's beautiful daughter, Alexandria. They begin a relationship, but her aunt cautions Jack about a woman losing her honor in Mexico. The Mexican authorities come to the ranch. They arrest Jack and Daniel and take them to the same prison at which Billy is incarcerated. Thereafter, Billy is executed.

"Jack and Daniel are released. Jack learns that his release was arranged by Alexandria's aunt on condition that he no longer contact Alexandria. He contacts her anyway and proposes marriage. She declines, as she must keep her promise to her family.

"The aunt is somewhat unfair with Jack as she prohibits him from seeing Alexandria because he is poor.

"Alexandria, compared to Conrad's other female characters, is relatively normal, as she comes from an upscale home, the horse ranch, and is being looked after by someone genuinely concerned about her well-being, or at least genuinely concerned about her image, her aunt."

Alley added, "Conrad sent me the manuscript for that book.

As I said before, the book is full of me but not me, and I was surprised that being written about did not feel good. I cried for days reading about Billy being executed. I felt violated."

Jason asked, "Do you think that your reaction might be a little melodramatic. This is perhaps the one book where the girl playing your part is not killed. She simply realizes that in her culture she cannot marry a person such as Jack as she has her reputation, and the reputation of her family, to protect."

Alley said, "But the book is about me, the horses and the ranch life. I was, perhaps, more idealized. Unlike me, the female character, Alexandria, had the creature comforts made available to a child when her family has money, and she has someone to look after her. I never had these things. But I believe that Conrad wanted this kind of life for me. I have horses now, so maybe it was not that far off."

Jason continues, "The next book is entitled *Cities of the Desert*. In it, Jack, the same Jack from *Wild Horses,* joins with another character from another of Conrad's books. They decide to work together on a cattle ranch in New Mexico.

"During a visit to a brothel in Juarez, Jack falls in love with a young, epileptic prostitute, Margarita. They decide to marry and live in the United States. The brothel is owned by Jorge. On the day that Jack and Margarita plan to cross the Rio Grande, Jorge has one of his associates murder Margarita by cutting her throat."

Alley said, "Here we had a perfectly innocent girl killed by having her throat cut with a knife. A very violent, but sad death."

Jason went on, "During his third marriage, it is said that Conrad's writing became softer. After the marriage failed in 2006, his writing returned to the dark side in his next book, *No Place for the Elderly.*

"In *No Place for the Elderly,* Tom, the husband, comes across a drug deal gone wrong and finds a brief case filled with 2 million dollars. He takes it home and tells his wife, Betty Jane, to go and stay with her mother, which she does. Anthony is hired to retrieve the money.

"Tom's mother-in-law accidentally tells the Mexicans where

he is located. Tom gives his wife the brief case for safekeeping. After the mother-in-law's funeral, Anthony is waiting for Betty Jane. It is uncertain whether he kills her or not. However, because he is mindful of the blood running towards his boot, the implication is that he does killer.

"Anthony makes this telling statement: 'Your husband had the opportunity to save you. But instead, he used you to save himself.'"

"When Tom and Betty Jane met, she was 16 and he was 33. She had a difficult relationship with her family and looked to Tom as her savior, not unlike you.

"The next writing was a screenplay called *The Attorney.* The Attorney partners with a drug dealer to enter into his first drug deal. After the plan is foiled, the Attorney is blamed, and his girlfriend, Lana, is kidnapped by the cartel. Lana is murdered, and her headless body is dumped into a landfill.

"The last two books, *The Diver* and *Sarah Gellar,* are companion works. They center around a brother and sister, Bobby and Alice Eastern. They are both math prodigies, and their father worked on the Manhattan Project to develop the atomic bomb.

"Both Alice and Bobby are conflicted over their father's contribution to the development of the bomb. Alice commits suicide 10 years prior to *The Diver* taking place. Bobby becomes a salvage diver but remains haunted by his father's work."

Chapter 12
The Interview

The Muse Factor

Jason postulated as follows: "Some people may take the position that you over-reacted to Conrad's writings and over-exaggerated your role in his life for your own benefit.

"In the various works, there are six primary women characters, Amanda, Alexandria, Margarita, Betty Jane, Lana, and Alice Eastern.

"In *The River,* Amanda was added as a character after you and Conrad met. She was underage, came from a poor background, and was killed by a landslide.

"In *Wild* Horses, Alexandria is the daughter of the ranch owner where Jack was working with the horses. She refuses Jack's offer of marriage to keep her promise to her family.

"In *Cities of the Desert,* Margarita is a prostitute who was killed with a knife by her pimp's associate before she could cross into the United States to marry Jack.

"In *No Place for the Elderly,* Betty Jane is the wife of Tom, the trapper who found a brief case with $2 million in cash which he gave to her to hold for safekeeping, getting her killed.

"In *The Attorney,* Lana, the fiancée of the Attorney, was killed by being beheaded when the Attorney, her boyfriend, is blamed for a failed drug deal.

"In *The Diver and Sarah Geller,* Alice Eastern is the daughter of one of the people involved in creating the atomic bomb; she committed suicide.

"When considering your role as Conrad's muse, as even I

see it, there are several similarities between your life and the life of his leading ladies and even the boys who, at least from my vantage point, should be considered.

"We know that Amanda and Betty Jane came from poor circumstances. We presume that Margarita, as she was working as a prostitute, probably came from poor circumstances. Though Alexandria was not from poor circumstances, the three boys, Jack, Daniel, and Billy, probably were. We presume that Betty Jane, who was working at Walmart when she met Tom, was probably from poor circumstances.

"At least two of the women, Amanda and Betty Jane, became involved with their older lovers when they were 16, similar to you and Conrad. Betty Jane looked up to Tom as her savior, similar to the way you may have looked up to Conrad.

"Betty Jane and Lana were each badly betrayed by their significant other. Betty Jane was given the cartel's money to hold which resulted in her being killed. Lana was killed over the cartel's money. Conrad's personal guilt for not forging a more permanent relationship with you may have caused him to see himself as a person who may have contributed to your demise.

"Margarita, before she could have a meaningful relationship with Jack, was stabbed to death with a knife by her pimp's accomplice. She was a woman who was held back from a permanent relationship by being killed.

"We see repeated elements of violent deaths. Yet, when you ask Conrad why he could not let Billy live in *No Place for the Elderly*, he brushes it off by saying that he is a writer and as a writer, his only alternative was for Billy to die.

"If we are looking for a most visceral and direct attack on you, or anyone else for that matter, Conrad offers up the most depraved act known to mankind: the act of suicide. Alice Eastern, racked with guilt about her father's involvement in the development of the atomic bomb, commits suicide. Still, ten years later, her brother continues to experience guilt over their father's work. But having Alice commit suicide was quite a personal, final, and horrible touch.

"Five of the six leading ladies in the six works were killed, and their deaths were primarily violent. The only woman to survive was Alexandria in *Wild Horses*, and she does so only because she listens to her older, and much wiser, aunt. The other ladies are on their own, and were betrayed by their male counter-parts."

Alley interrupted Jason's long rant and said, "That is all very interesting. And I can tell you in no uncertain terms that when I read these various works, I was depressed and felt as if they were somehow aimed at me. I saw no element of romance in being written about in the manners chosen by Conrad.

"Maybe I meant less to him than I wish to admit. I will say that whenever we were together after the break up, I always felt as if he was with me only to try to find more background for his characters."

Jason replied, "Fair enough. I know that very late in his life you wrote a comment to a review of *The Diver* which I thought was telling. It was so moving I kept it. May I read it?"

Alley replied, "If you feel you must."

Jason started, "The comment written by you said: 'Santa Fe killed the Conrad I knew. He gained fame, wealth, and fancy superficial friends. He turned his back on his old friends like Jimmy Long (J-Bone) and Billy Kidwell. They were left to die, forgotten and alone. He lost much of his compassion and kindness. As the Institute crowd claimed more of his time, he struggled to write. Couldn't write. How could he? He's stifled or killed that which inspired him. The advance for *The Diver* was spent. He was obligated. These last many years he has taken up drinking again. Living in majestic splendor but enjoying none of it. Surrounded by junk and the clutter of a lifetime. Haunted.'"

Jason then asked, "Did you allow him the opportunity to read this?"

Alley replied, "I did more than that; I read it to him."

Jason asked, "Did he have a reply?"

Alley replied, "Oh, yes. To heighten the effect, I will quote to you verbatim exactly what he said to me. He said: 'Well, you pretty much laid it all out, didn't you?'"

Jason said, "I agree with you when you say that you were not pleased that he used your likeness in his stories without your consent or without even consulting you. I agree that seeing yourself splashed across the pages of his works, could not have been good, and very well may have led you to the depression of which you have spoken.

"I agree that receiving love letters, particularly with explicit content, from someone with whom one is not, at the time of receipt, romantically involved could be troubling.

"He married three other women and had children with two of them. One was even separated from him by more years than you and he were separated. He backed out of two marriage proposals to you. You had, by all accounts, a short, unsuccessful marriage."

Alley asked, "So, you think I was jealous?"

Jason replied, "I don't know if I would use that term, but were you?"

Alley asked, "I can't say, but I know for sure that I was at least a little miffed. Is that it. Are we done?"

Justin replied, "If you would like us to be done, we can be done."

Alley replied, "Yes, I think so. You did a very thorough job. Perhaps more thorough than anyone else might have been. I've learned much about Conrad, his writing, his characters, and the motivation of his characters.

"I see how some readers relate to my involvement while others do not relate to me at all, when it comes to Conrad. Frankly, it has been difficult for me to accept that his characters could relate to anyone other than I.

"Perhaps I have been selfish, or at least foolish. I have read many articles about Conrad. In some, the relationship with me has been mentioned. In others, our relationship has not even been addressed at all.

"I know that much of what Conrad and I shared found its way into his books, even if biographers and reviewers could not see it, or do not mention it.

"Perhaps to them whatever involvement I had in Conrad's productive life was not important or was very minor. How could such a no-body inspire such a great writer, they ask.

"But coming to grips with being considered to have been outside of his productive life may be more difficult than coming to grips with being too large a part of it, his muse, if you will.

"This has been a fascinating exercise. I have learned not only much about Conrad and his works, but I have learned much about myself.

"Thank you for all of your hard work and research."

Justin concluded, "No, thank you for being such a forthcoming subject."

About the Author

Tighe Taylor is a graduate of Whittier College, School of Law, located in Los Angeles County, California. He lives and works in Los Angeles where he owns a consulting business and practices law. His prior literary works include the non-fiction book entitled *The Tragic Death of Marina Habe,* a true crime account of the most unfortunate kidnapping and murder of Marina Habe, a childhood friend. The next four books are crime fiction. They include *The Kidnapping of Tammy Fitzgerald, Second Edition, The Kidnapping of Taylor Shaw, The Kidnapping of Isabel Miller,* and *The Kidnapping of Crystal Covington.* The kidnapping series follows the travails of Taylor Shaw. Ms. Shaw starts out as a down-on-her-luck farm girl who works her way up through the system to become a lawyer and, eventually, Woman of the Year. After these books, the author returns to non-fiction with *The Constitutional Convention, How Political Parties and No Term Limits Shattered the Dreams of the Founders (and other stories).* In his present offering, the author continues in the non-fiction genre with *The Federal Reserve, Audit, Amend, or Abolish.* This book includes a work of fiction entitled *The Muse, A Short Story*, about an author inspired by his muse.

www.ingramcontent.com/pod-product-compliance
Lightning Source LLC
LaVergne TN
LVHW041706060526
838201LV00043B/600